The Governance of Regulators

Driving Performance at Peru's Telecommunications Regulator

Please cite this publication as:
OECD (2019), *Driving Performance at Peru's Telecommunications Regulator*, The Governance of Regulators, OECD Publishing, Paris.
https://doi.org/10.1787/9789264310506-en

ISBN 978-92-64-31049-0 (print)
ISBN 978-92-64-31050-6 (pdf)
ISBN 978-92-64-31051-3 (HTML)
ISBN 978-92-64-31052-0 (epub)

Series: The Governance of Regulators
ISSN 2415-1432 (print)
ISSN 2415-1440 (online)

Photo credits: Cover © Leigh Prather - Fotolia.com, © Mr.Vander - Fotolia.com, © magann - Fotolia.com.

Corrigenda to OECD publications may be found on line at: *www.oecd.org/about/publishing/corrigenda.htm*.

Foreword

Economic regulators should play an important role as impartial referees to guarantee the predictability and certainty of regulatory regimes – crucial features for attracting investment. Their job is inherently a complex one, requiring neutral engagement with a variety of actors, including government, citizens and consumers, and operators. The model of independent economic regulation, based on strong technical capacity, transparency, autonomy and constructive engagement with stakeholders, can help, tackle this complex landscape. Moreover, independent regulators can provide certainty to markets and society during periods of external instability. Regulators need to be correctly equipped, however, to carry out these fundamental tasks and stay abreast of market evolutions.

To support regulators as they face these challenges, the OECD has developed a framework to assess and strengthen their organisational performance and governance structures. The framework analyses regulators' internal and external governance, including their organisational structures, behaviour, accountability, business processes, reporting and performance management, as well as role clarity, relationships, distribution of powers and responsibilities with other government and non-government stakeholders.

This report applies this Performance Assessment Framework to Peru's telecommunications regulator (Supervisory Agency for Private Investment in Telecommunications, *Organismo Supervisor de Inversión Privada en Telecomunicaciones*, OSIPTEL). The review finds that OSIPTEL enjoys a strong internal culture and commitment to delivering on its mandate, but needs to better promote the overall benefits of independent economic regulation externally.

As one of four economic regulators created in the 1990s, OSIPTEL has overseen the transformation of Peru's telecommunications sector and market into a diverse and competitive market benefitting the country's citizens and businesses. Stakeholders view the regulator as a technically sound body that has delivered on its mandate over the years. The review finds, however, that there is still scope to improve several areas linked to the regulator's governance. These include building more robust and diverse internal decision making mechanisms, including at the level of the Board of Directors, strengthening transparency and integrity processes, and engaging with stakeholders more regularly to report on regulator and sector performance.

Moreover, a more proactive external relations strategy could contribute to a better understanding of the role of the regulator externally and could mitigate risks linked to external factors. This strategy should aim to build a "no surprises" relationship with stakeholders and could, in the medium term, lay the groundwork for solutions to some structural challenges faced by OSIPTEL such as ensuring that appropriate functions, resource frameworks and coordination mechanisms are in place. Finally, the review, carried out in parallel with that of the Peru's energy and mining regulator, Osinergmin, recommends that Peru's four economic regulators work together more effectively to share best practices and address common challenges.

These actions, among others put forward in this report, could help OSIPTEL build on its technical work and reputation to become an example of institutional maturity within the Peruvian public administration.

This report is part of the OECD work programme on the governance of regulators and regulatory policy, led by the OECD Network of Economic Regulators and the OECD Regulatory Policy Committee, with the support of the Regulatory Policy Division of the OECD Directorate of Public Governance. The Directorate's mission is to help government at all levels design and implement strategic, evidence-based and innovative policies that support sustainable economic and social development.

Acknowledgements

This report was co-ordinated and prepared by Anna Pietikainen and James Drummond. The work underlying the report was led by Filippo Cavassini. Substantive comments were provided by Lorenzo Casullo, Filippo Cavassini, Andrea Perez, Winona Rei Bolislis, as well as Nick Malyshev, Head of the Regulatory Policy Division. The work received encouragement and support of Marcos Bonturi, Director, and Irène Hors, Deputy Director, Public Governance Directorate. Jennifer Stein co-ordinated the editorial process and Kate Lancaster and Andrea Uhrhammer provided editorial support. Alejandro Camacho of the OECD Mexico Centre provided support for the translation of the report into Spanish, which was prepared by Solar Servicios Editoriales.

The team included three peer reviewers from the members of the OECD Network of Economic Regulators (NER), who participated in a policy mission to Ireland and provided extensive inputs and feedback throughout the development of the review: Ms. Luisa Perrotti, former Head of Cabinet, Presidency, Transport Regulation Authority (ART), Italy; Mr. Adolfo Cuevas, Commissioner, Federal Telecommunications Institute (IFT), Mexico; and Mr. Jonathan Porter, Senior Economic Advisor, Ofcom, United Kingdom.

The report would not have been possible without the support of OSIPTEL and its staff. The team would in particular like to thank the following colleagues for their unique assistance in collecting data and information, organising the team's missions to Peru and providing feedback at different stages of the development of the review: Rafael Muente, President of the Board; Sergio Cifuentes, General Manager; Romina Alania, Management Specialist; Vanessa Castillo, International Affairs Coordinator; and Claudio Palomares, International Relations Specialist. Interviews and comments from the various OSIPTEL departments, government, industry and public stakeholders during the review process also contributed to the analysis presented in the report.

A draft of the report was discussed at the OECD Network of Economic Regulators in November 2018.

Table of contents

Tables

Figures

Boxes

Acronyms and abbreviations

CEPLAN	National Centre for Strategic Planning (*Centro Nacional de Planeamiento estratégico*)
CGR	Comptroller General of the Republic of Peru (*Contraloría General de la República del Perú*)
CPP	Peruvian Political Constitution (*Constitución Política del Perú*)
CODECO	Commission for Consumer Defence and Regulators of Public Utilities (*Comisión Defensa del Consumidor y Organismos Reguladores de los Servicios Públicos*)
ERESTEL	Annual Consumer Demand Survey (*Encuesta residencial de servicios de telecomunicaciones*)
FITEL	Telecommunications Investment Fund (*Fondo de Inversión en Telecomunicaciones*)
GAF	Administration and Finance Department (*Gerencia de Administración y Finanzas*)
GAL	Legal Advisory Department (*Gerencia Asesoría Legal*)
GOD	Decentralised Offices Department (*Gerencia de Oficinas Desconcentradas*)
GPP	Planning and Budget Department (*Gerencia de Planeamiento y Presupuesto*)
GPRC	Regulatory Policy and Competition Department (*Gerencia de Políticas Regulatorias y Competencia*)
GPSU	Protection and User Services Department (*Gerencia de Protección y Servicio al Usuario*)
GSF	Enforcement and Supervision Department (*Gerencia de Supervisión y Fiscalización*)
Indecopi	National Institute for the Defense of Competition and Intellectual Property (*Instituto Nacional de Defensa de la Competencia y Protección de la Propiedad Intelectual*)
ISO	International Organisation for Standardisation
LMOR	Framework Law on Regulatory Agencies for Private Investment in Public Utilities (*Ley Marco de los Organismos Reguladores de la Inversión Privada en los Servicios Públicos*)
LOGR	Organic Law of Regional Governments (*Ley Orgánica de Gobiernos Regionales*)
LOM	Organic Law of Municipalities (*Ley Orgánica de Municipalidades*)
LOPE	Organic Law of the Executive Power (*Ley Orgánica del Poder Ejecutivo*)
MCRQ	Multi-Sectoral Commission on Regulatory Quality (*Comisión Multisectorial de Calidad Regulatoria*)

MEF	Ministry of Economy and Finance (*Ministerio de Economía y Finanzas*)
MINJUS	Ministry of Justice and Human Rights (*Ministerio de Justicia y Derechos Humanos*)
MTC	Ministry of Transport and Communications (*Ministerio de Tranporte y Comunicaciones*)
NER	Network of Economic Regulators
NRIP	Periodic Information Requirements Rule (*Norma de Requerimientos de Información Periódica*)
PAFER	Performance Assessment Framework for Economic Regulators
PCM	Presidency of the Council of Ministers (*Presidencia del Consejo de Ministros*)
PEDN	National Strategic Development Plan (*Plan Estratégico de Desarrollo Nacional*)
PEI	Strategic Institutional Plan (*Plan Estratégico Institucional*)
POI	Operational Institutional Plan (*Objetivos Estratégicos Institucionales*)
Prolnversión	Agency for the Promotion of Investment (*Agencia de Promoción de la Inversión Privada,* Prolnversión)
OCI	Institutional Control Body (*Órgano de Control Institucional*)
Osinergmin	Supervisory Agency for Investment in Energy and Mining (*Organismo Supervisor de la Inversión en Energía y Minería*)
OSIPTEL	Supervisory Agency for Private Investment in Telecommunications (*Organismo Supervisor de Inversión Privada en Telecomunicaciones*)
OSITRAN	Supervisory Agency for Investment in Public Transport Infrastructure (*Organismo Supervisor de la Inversión en Infraestructura de Transporte de Uso Público*)
RDNFO	National Fibre Optical Backbone (*Red Dorsal Nacional de Fibra Optica*)
RIA	Regulatory Impact Assessment
RQA	Regulatory Quality Assessment
SERVIR	National Civil Service Authority (*Autoridad Nacional del Servicio Civil*)
SIAF	Integrated Administrative Financial System (*Sistemas integrados de administación financiera*)
SIGEP	Periodic Information System (*Sistema de gestión de las estadísticas periódicas*)
SINAPLAN	National System of Strategic Planning (*Sistema Nacional de Planeamiento Estratégico*)
SIRT	Price Information System (*Sistema de consultas de tarifas*)
SUNASS	National Superintendence of Sanitation Services (*Superintendencia Nacional de Servicios de Saneamiento*)
TRASU	Administrative court for the resolution of user complaints (*Tribunal Administrativo de Solución de Reclamos de Usuarios*)

Executive summary

The Supervisory Agency for Private Investment in Telecommunications (Organismo *Supervisor de Inversión Privada en Telecomunicaciones*, OSIPTEL) was created as Peru's regulator for the telecommunications sector in 1994. Since then, the regulator has overseen the liberalisation of the market and the transformation of services offered to the country's citizens and businesses via new technologies. While OSIPTEL has enjoyed a stable mandate, the dynamism and pace of change in the telecommunications sector have increased its regulatory functions. To adapt successfully to these new challenges, the regulator will need to strengthen its external relations strategy, create a more predictable framework for stakeholder engagement and results reporting, and enhance internal governance and clarity in decision making.

Role and objectives

OSIPTEL is a specialised and decentralised regulatory body with technical, administrative, economic and financial autonomy. However like all Peruvian economic regulators, it relies on the Presidency of the Council of Ministers (*Presidencia del Consejo de Ministros,* PCM) for approval for several procedures and is subject to public finance rules. It operates within sector policy set by the executive and regularly publishes non-binding technical opinions in response to Ministry consultations. There are no formal or structured co-ordination mechanisms bringing together public entities intervening in the telecommunications sector.

OSIPTEL has enjoyed a stable mandate and developed a strong reputation as a technically competent body with strong internal culture and commitment to delivering on its mandate. The regulator sets its strategic objectives in four-year strategic plans and has an active communications and outreach strategy.

Key recommendations

- ***Build*** a "no surprises" relationship with stakeholders based on enhanced engagement and trust, including via a robust external relations strategy focusing on the core objectives and results of the regulator, more active sector co-ordination mechanisms and joint efforts among economic regulators to address common opportunities and challenges.
- ***Assess*** whether the functions and powers of the regulator are aligned with its role and objectives, taking into account distribution of powers with other public entities as well as international best practice.
- ***Share*** OSIPTEL methodology on strategic planning with other public entities and use this as a basis for building stable forward regulatory planning.

Input

OSIPTEL is entirely funded by resources received from the regulated sector. In practice, its budget has been limited by central government rules that cap the amount received from the sector below what is allowed by legislation, as well as by austerity measures, leaving the regulator feeling under-resourced and unable to manage its funds freely.

OSIPTEL is recognised as having highly skilled technical staff, but does not have a uniform recruitment framework. Despite the constraints of the government employment framework, OSIPTEL is generally viewed as a desirable place to work thanks to a number of successful initiatives implemented by management.

Key recommendations

- ***Review*** regulatory fees on a regular basis based on cost recovery principles and seek clarity on central administration constraints on the regulator's funding model and financial management.
- ***Implement*** a human resources framework for diversity, recruitment, remuneration and incentives that takes into account the special needs of economic regulators, including levelling the playing field in terms of recruitment practices and contract frameworks.

Process

Decision making at OSIPTEL is led by the Board of Directors, which operates under a wide executive mandate, provides little input to strategic questions, and with limited resources. Internal management is centralised in the President of the Board and General Manager.

OSIPTEL uses good regulatory practices to improve the quality of regulations. It was a pioneer in the Peruvian administration for the implementation of regulatory impact assessments (RIAs) for all regulatory decisions. However, stakeholder engagement tends to happen late in the process, and *ex post* reviews are not systematically conducted. While OSIPTEL places a high priority on transparent and accountable decision making, sharing information on sector performance and its activities, it lacks formal accountability mechanisms.

Key recommendations

- ***Assess*** whether the Board's activities and resources are aligned with its mandate, and introduce internal quality control and challenge functions.
- ***Create*** an advisory committee of stakeholders for transparent and early consultation with industry, users, and other relevant stakeholders to enhance the inclusiveness and predictability of OSIPTEL's regulatory activities.
- ***Put*** in place a regular engagement activity with the Congress to increase accountability and promote understanding of the regulator's role and activities by the legislature.

Output and outcome

OSIPTEL's activities are guided by a five-year strategic framework, which includes a mix of outcome and organisational goals, supported by sophisticated indicators to measure their achievement. However, monitoring these indicators is resource intensive, and the results are under-utilised for accountability and transparency purposes. The regulator collects and publishes large amounts of raw data, as well as a variety of reports using this data.

Key recommendations

- ***Further*** align the annual report to the strategic framework and use it as an opportunity to communicate on achievements against the strategic objectives.
- ***Organise*** a public event with stakeholders to present the annual report.
- ***Explore*** opportunities to streamline or reduce data-reporting requirements to improve the consistency and completeness of the information, and review data collection processes.

Assessment and recommendations

Since its creation in 1994, OSIPTEL has enjoyed a stable mandate over a dynamic and rapidly evolving market as economic regulator for the telecommunications sector, and is commended by stakeholders as a technically competent body. It was created alongside three other economic regulators in the 1990s to oversee Peru's transition to a liberalised economy and provide long-term stability over key economic sectors. Over 20 years, the telecommunications sector and market has evolved into a diverse and competitive market, which has benefitted the country's citizens and businesses. As part of this evolution, the functions of the regulator have increased as new have been roles and responsibilities added by the executive and legislature and the range of communications services, and methods for delivering them, have continued to grow. The regulator enjoys a strong internal culture and commitment to delivering on its mandate.

As a result, there is scope for OSIPTEL to invest in several areas linked to its internal and external governance as a means towards bolstering its institutional and organisational capacity to provide certainty to markets and society. This includes building more robust and diverse internal decision-making mechanisms, including at the level of the Board of Directors, strengthening transparency and integrity processes, as well as engaging with stakeholders more regularly to report on regulator and sector performance. A more proactive external relations strategy implemented by the regulator could contribute to a better understanding of its role externally and could mitigate risks linked to external instability. This strategy should aim to cement a "no surprises" relationship with stakeholders and could, in the medium term, lay the groundwork for finding solutions to more systemic challenges faced by OSIPTEL. Working more effectively with Peru's other economic regulators to share best practices from their operations and address shared challenges can help amplify effects and establish these regulatory agencies as examples of institutional maturity within the Peruvian public administration.

Role and objectives

Mandate

OSIPTEL is one of four economic regulators created in the 1990s to oversee Peru's transition to a liberalised economy. The regulator shares a legal framework (*Ley marco de los organismos reguladores de la inversión privada en los servicios públicos*, Law 27332, or LMOR) with the other economic regulators that grants them autonomy but places them under the aegis of the Presidency of the Council of Ministers (*Presidencia del Consejo de Ministros*, PCM). The LMOR establishes OSIPTEL and its fellow sector regulators (energy and mining, transport, water) as specialised and decentralised regulatory bodies with technical, administrative, economic and financial autonomy. However, sector regulators depend on the PCM for approval of several procedures, from changes in organisational structure to international travel of staff, which may hinder rapid and effective decision-making and intervention, as well as create challenges to the independence of the regulator along specific pinch points in its life cycle.

OSIPTEL has enjoyed a stable mandate over a dynamic and rapidly evolving market since its creation as Peru's economic regulator for the telecommunications sector in 1994. Created by the Legislative Decree No. 702 in 1991 and officially starting operations in 1994, OSIPTEL oversaw the liberalisation of the telecommunications market over its first years of operation (see Table 1). By law, its objectives are to guarantee the quality and efficiency of services to the user and to regulate sector tariffs. OSIPTEL also regulates and supervises competition and consumer protection in the telecommunication market, a function exercised exclusively by the National Institute for the Defense of Competition and Intellectual Property (*Instituto Nacional de Defensa de la Competencia y Protección de la Propiedad Intelectual*, Indecopi), Peru's competition and consumer protection authority, for most other sectors of Peru's economy. This mandate is reflected in the regulator's current slogan: *promovemos la competencia y empoderamos al usuario* (we promote competition and empower the user). Since 1994, the telecommunications market has evolved from one state company to 5 large operators and more than 100 small- and medium-sized enterprises in 2018, as well as introduced mobile telephony, mobile and fixed internet, pay TV and fibre internet to the market to the benefit of Peru's citizens and economy.

Table 1. OSIPTEL powers and functions

Competition	Promotes competition between telecommunications operators by reducing barriers to entry and costs for consumers to switch providers
Tariff-setting	Sets tariffs for public utilities in the telecommunications sector
Regulatory	Establishes norms and rules, define infractions and set sanctions;
Inspections and enforcement	Qualifies infractions and impose sanctions
Conflict resolution	Resolves disputes in telecommunications sector
Claim resolution	Acts as second instance for customer claims
Supervisory	Supervises that regulated entities respect sector norms and regulations emitted by the regulator

Source: (OSIPTEL, 2018[1]).

While the regulator enjoys a strong internal culture and commitment to delivering on its mandate, there is a need to make the case for independent economic regulation externally. Independent economic regulators provide certainty and predictability through medium- to long-term strategic visions and the regulatory regimes that they develop and uphold. Over time, this inspires trust in public institutions and encourages investment. The independence of regulators and their capacity to make evidence-based technical decisions gives regulators the potential to act as bulwarks against undue influence and corruption, increasing trust in the public administration. These benefits of independent economic regulation are relevant and valuable to the Peruvian political context that has been mired by instability linked to corruption scandals in 2017-18.

A more proactive external relations strategy can help stakeholders understand the role and benefits of independent economic regulation and help tackle external risks. A robust external relations strategy, built around communicating the core contributions and impact of economic regulators on the economy, would provide a counterweight to the instability that is outside of the control of the regulatory authority. While independence is important, it does not mean that regulators act in isolation; on the contrary, such a strategy should aim for constructive engagement, setting up an on-going dialogue and building trust. The impact could be amplified by implementing such a strategy jointly, when relevant, with Peru's other economic regulators. It could contribute to the better understanding of the role of the regulator and the construction of a "no surprises" relationship with other branches of government and the regulated sector that could lay the foundation for addressing more structural shortcomings when the time is right.

Box 1. Examples of co-ordination among regulatory agencies

The challenges faced by regulators often transcend sectoral and geographical boundaries; hence, greater co-ordination and collaboration are needed. There are a number of experiences with co-ordination among regulatory agencies domestically, including:

Australia: the Utility Regulators Forum aims to facilitate the exchange of information, understanding of the issues faced by regulators, consistency in the application of regulatory functions and the review of new ideas about regulatory practices. The newsletter of the forum is published quarterly and contains articles on common challenges, summaries of recent journal articles on regulatory matters, and updates on regulatory decisions.

France: the *Club des Régulateurs* provides a forum for both established and new economic regulators to share common problems with a few thematic meetings every year, most recently on issues of data privacy and data handling. It is hosted by a third party, currently an academic institution.

Mexico: following the OECD's peer review of three energy regulators (Agency for Safety, Energy and Environment, ASEA; National Hydrocarbons Commission, CNH; and Energy Regulatory Commission, CRE), a permanent co-ordination group for the energy sector was established, leading to joint briefs, inspections and an exchange programme, better equipping regulators to implement wide-ranging sector reforms.

United Kingdom (Scotland): As part of the Strategic Review of charges for 2021-2027, stakeholders in Scotland meet on a monthly basis to ensure collective buy-in and collaborative working around the key issues faced by the water and wastewater sectors. The meetings involve high-level representatives from the water operator (Scottish Water), economic regulator (The Water Industry Commission for Scotland, WICS), the quality regulator (Drinking Water Quality Regulator for Scotland, DWQR) and the environment regulator (Scottish Environment Protection Agency, SEPA), as well as the Customer Forum and the consumers association. More granular analysis from the working groups feeds into those high-level discussions.

Source: Network of Economic Regulators (NER) at the OECD, 2018.

Recommendations:

- ***Develop*** a robust external relations strategy that communicates the core objectives, raison d'être and results of the regulator, and, when relevant, do so jointly with Peru's other economic regulators. This external relations strategy would provide a stable narrative on the work of OSIPTEL by focusing on a limited number of key indicators / results and could be communicated by all members of the board and senior management. This strategy and the resources for its implementation would be differentiated from communication activities aiming at implementing OSIPTEL function of customer protection and sharing information relative to user rights.

- ***Set up*** a forum where economic regulators of Peru can come together with the objective of harmonising messages on the role of economic regulators and jointly advocating for governance-related topics as relevant. The forum would not minimise the need for sectoral focus in the technical work of the regulators and it could, as relevant, also be open to other public agencies in charge of competition, customer or environmental protection, safety, etc. The chairmanship of the group could rotate between the regulatory authorities and the group should aim to focus on concrete deliverable and activities, rather than setting up a bureaucratic system of collaboration.
- ***Develop*** stable yearly regulatory planning linked to a strong strategic framework and a vision that promotes the mandate of the regulator. This regulatory plan should be transparently and predictably shared with all stakeholders to favour inclusive and effective participation in stakeholder engagement.

Box 2. Example of transparent regulatory planning with the Australian Competition and Consumer Commission (ACCC)

The ACCC post on its website its compliance and enforcement policy and priorities, which includes priorities for the calendar year as well as enduring priorities for forms of conduct considered so detrimental to consumer welfare and competitive processes that the ACCC will always regard them as a priority. The policy statement includes details about the principles and approaches underlying the policy, the compliance and enforcement strategy, priority factors, compliance activities, enforcement actions, and market studies. A section is also included for co-ordination with other government agencies.

Source: (ACCC, 2018[2]).

Institutional co-ordination

OSIPTEL operates within sector policy set by the executive and regularly publishes technical opinions in response to Ministry consultations but its submissions are not binding. Policy for the telecommunications sector is set by the Ministry of Transport and Telecommunications (*Ministerio de Telecomunicaciones y Transporte,* MTC) as per article 75 of the Telecommunications Law, approved by Supreme Decree No. 013-93-TCC (1993). In general, communication between the regulator and the line ministry is constructive and fluid, and by law MTC can solicit technical support from the regulator. OSIPTEL does this regularly and informally before open consultations, relying on the regulator's high level of technical expertise and capacity. Both institutions can provide comments to the other's open consultations. However, OSIPTEL's technical opinions on Ministry consultations are non-binding in nature and in some instances the Ministry has acted contrary to the regulator's recommendations.

A number of Peruvian public entities intervene in the telecommunications sector, but there are no formal and structured co-ordination mechanisms, undermining a harmonised and stable vision for the sector (see Table 2). Several entities of the executive branch as well as Peru's unicameral Congress can initiate activities that will impact the regulator's duties and functions. These range, for example, from national security policy by the Ministry of Interior or the national data policy by the Ministry of

Justice, to legislations passed by Congress that will require the regulator to pass corresponding secondary legislation. No structured co-ordination mechanisms exist that would bring together these entities to share and align plans and activities in the telecommunications sector. On the one hand, this can contribute to a perceived lack of uniform policy and vision for the sector while, on the other, create excessive burdens on regulated entities. It can also erode the clarity of roles between the different entities. In a context of instability and unpredictability this can also lead to an inefficient and ineffective allocation of resources, when efforts focus on short-term reactive activities, instead of implementing a deliberate medium to long-term strategic vision and objectives.

Table 2. Peruvian public bodies involved in the telecommunications sector or the regulator

Institution	Role	Interactions with OSIPTEL
Congress	Unicameral legislative branch of 130 members.	Has the power to request OSIPTEL to provide comments on issues or draft laws in either full plenary or in two standing committees – the Transport and Communications Committee and the Defense of Consumers and Regulatory Bodies Commission (CODECO)
Presidency of the Council of Ministers (PCM)	Responsible for co-ordinating national and sectoral policies within the executive branch	Oversees and provides guidance on the general administrative processes, key role in nominating and appointing Board members, administering budget allocations and disbursements.
Ministry of Economy and Finance (MEF)	Developing economic and financial policy for Peru, including co-ordinating the performance-budgeting system	OSIPTEL must report on indicators regard their yearly operational plan (*Plan Operativo Institucional*, POI) through the performance-budgeting system
Ministry of Transport and Communications (MTC)	Defining and developing policies for Peru's transportation systems and telecommunications sector	MTC established general sector policy, as well as performs some regulatory and supervisory functions, and oversees various projects, such as the Telecommunications Investment Fund (FITEL). Can request OSIPTEL to provide comments on issues or draft laws and regulations.
Telecommunications Investment Fund (FITEL)	Subsidises the installation, operation and use of public telecommunications services in rural areas and is funded by levies on service operators and carriers as well as fines collected from supervisions	OSIPTEL participates in non-binding discussions related to investments and supervises contracts
Proinversión	Specialised technical body attached to the MEF responsible for the promotion of national investments through public-private partnerships (PPPs) in services, infrastructure, assets, and other state projects	Can receive non-binding comments from OSIPTEL when developing investment projects
Indecopi	Independent regulatory body aimed at both providing competition and consumer protection.	Has the authority to issue binding decisions and levy penalties on regulators or decisions taken by OSIPTEL, as well as conduct *ex post* reviews of regulations enacted by OSIPTEL and under the jurisdiction of Indecopi.
Ministry of Interior	Oversees issues related to national security, including civil defense	New national security laws have recently given the Ministry requirements and authority to promote national and cross-border network and telecommunications security
Ministry of Justice	Oversees judicial matters in Peru	Oversees the role of the courts, including the process of appeals and judicial review through which OSIPTEL's actions can be challenged. Proposes an attorney general for all public institutions.

Source: Prepared by the OECD Based on information collected during the review, 2018.

In addition to the role played by the Ministry, OSIPTEL provides support to the high-level policy goal of bridging the urban/rural divide through its work with the Telecommunications Investment Fund (*Fondo de Inversión en Telecommunicaciones,* FITEL). The fund is sourced from 1% of the gross income of service operators as well as from fines collected for non-compliance or violations (in 2017, its investment budget was USD 120 million). It finances the installation, operation, and use of public communications services in rural areas to achieve universal access. The fund was initially administered by OSIPTEL and was transferred to the Ministry of Transport and Communications (MTC) in 2006. The Board of FITEL is chaired by the Minister and composed of the Minister of Economy and Finance and the President of the Board of OSIPTEL. Projects are deployed using either Public-Private Partnerships (PPPs) or Project in Assets (*Proyectos en Activos*) framework. For projects implemented under the latter scheme, OSIPTEL cannot issue binding opinions over issues that intersect with their competencies, i.e. concession contracts, tariffs, quality of service, essential facilities, and competition. Moreover, for telecommunications projects implemented under this scheme, responsibility for supervising the quality of services is assigned to FITEL, which can run the risk of duplicating efforts with OSIPTEL who supervise quality of service in all other areas of the telecommunications sector. OSIPTEL can also be tasked with creating ad hoc regulations in accordance with specific projects.

Recommendations:

- ***Actively*** push for the creation and implementation of more structured and regular co-ordination mechanisms where all Peruvian entities with responsibilities and activities that impact the telecommunications sector would participate to share information, in the interest of building a "no surprises" relationship between all stakeholders. Such a mechanism would favour greater clarity of roles and enable robust forward planning by the regulator and its partners. This more high level engagement between senior management of the regulator and other branches of government, including Congress, should not replace more technical level collaboration between teams across public administration.
- ***Use*** reputation as strong and independent technical body to proactively share a strategic view on the sector, share advisory comments with the Ministry on the direction of the sector, publish comments submitted to consultations launched by other public bodies, and set up co-ordination mechanisms with stakeholders (i.e. advisory body) to share data and analysis on sector performance and what it means for the further development of the sector.
- ***Assess*** with the Ministry whether the governance and implementation of FITEL is aligned with overall strategic vision for the telecommunications sector, including optimising the role for OSIPTEL and co-operation between the regulator and the MTC at each stage of FITEL projects to ensure market distortions and unnecessary administrative burdens are not created and overlaps in functions are minimised.

Functions

The functions of the regulator have increased significantly over the years, linked to the evolution of the sector, while the Ministry still retains some central functions relative to the economic regulation of the sector. OSIPTEL estimates that since 2013, it has been granted 14 new functions linked to legislative texts originated by the legislative or executive branches without additional resources for their implementation. OSIPTEL expended PEN 5.5 million of their budget in 2017 on these new functions. Given the dynamism of the sector, it is likely that this trend carries on as the range of electronic communications services and the means of delivering them continues to grow. Moreover, the MTC retains key functions linked to the development and competition of the telecommunications sector. These include the licensing of new operators, decisions on structural separation and on spectrum allocation, the latter of which is designed and run by Proinversión. Some of these functions may be better addressed by an independent and technical regulator to ensure independent decision-making based on technical assessment. In some instances, the MTC has also come forward with instructions on tariffs and interconnection issues that fall under OSIPTEL functions. While OSIPTEL can submit and publish its opinions on MTC decisions in these areas, these opinions are non-binding and can be disregarded by MTC for the final decision. For instance, in the case of decisions by MTC on mergers with spectrum transfer, since 2015, OSIPTEL has issued opinions disagreeing with the transfer in all seven cases. In only one of these cases has the transfer not been approved by MTC; in all other cases the final decision has disregarded the regulator's opinion (Table 2.6).

The increased focus of OSIPTEL on the promotion of user satisfaction, in addition to ensuring consumer protection, is taking its toll on OSIPTEL resources and raises a concern of balance between its functions. Customer protection is one of the main objectives and functions of the regulator since its creation. Over the last years, an increased focus of the regulator on user protection and satisfaction has mostly been visible in OSIPTEL's function as second instance appeals body for customer claims through the Administrative court for the resolution of user complaints (*Tribunal Administrativo de Solución de Reclamos de Usuarios*, TRASU). This dispute resolution body processes claims that have not been successful or resolved with the operator. User complaints have risen exponentially since 2015 (by 68% 2015-16 and by 71% 2016-17, see Table 3), undoubtedly in part to being able to defer payment of a bill by presenting a complaint. As a result of the strain on OSIPTEL resources, the treatment time of second instance complaints has risen from 8-10 days in 2015 to 120 days in 2017. The number of complaints has started to decrease in 2018 following an adjustment of the corresponding regulation by OSIPTEL and will need to continue to be monitored (Table 3). Finally, the focus of the regulator and its resources user satisfaction overall may be misaligned with the structure of the market that it oversees. This function and objective may be more suitable in the case of monopolies and no longer valid in the case of a competitive market.

Table 3. Evolution of customer complaints

	2015	2016	2017	2018*
First instance complaints	1 273 780	2 133 958	3 647 026	1 636 258
Second instance on average* (TRASU)	31 226	59 047	159 371	14 643

Notes: OSIPTEL reports that, on average, 3.5% of first instance complaints move to second instance appeals with TRASU. 2018 statistics are as of June 2018.
Source: Information provided by OSIPTEL, 2018.

OSIPTEL's decentralised offices are responsible for interacting with subnational government and the public on a daily basis. The 23 regional offices and 8 centres across the country are responsible for handling local issues, measuring service quality, promoting user rights, and providing training to local enterprises. The centres share facilities with other decentralised public bodies. Regional offices are overseen by the Decentralised Offices Department (*Gerencia de Oficinas Desconcentradas*, GOD), Enforcement and Supervision Department (Gerencia de Supervisión y Fiscalización, GSF), and the Protection and User Services Department (*Gerencia de Protección y Servicio al Usuario*, GPSU) of OSIPTEL. Regional offices interact directly with local governments when resolving issues and co-ordinate with other relevant local offices, such as Osinergmin with regard to power failures that affect telecommunications service. In addition to advocacy, staff in regional offices deal with face-to-face interactions with consumers, notably with regard to complaint resolution.

Box 3. Functions and powers of Mexico's Federal Telecommunications Institute (IFT)

The IFT is the economic regulator and competition authority for the telecommunication and broadcasting sectors in Mexico. The IFT has the following powers:

a) The licensing, revocation, as well as the authorisation of assignments or changes to the shareholding control, ownership or operation of companies related to concessions in matters of broadcasting and telecommunications. The IFT sets the amount of compensation for granting of the concessions.

b) Imposing impose asymmetric measures upon dominant/preponderant players in telecommunication and broadcasting sectors, including the possibility of functional, structural or accounting separation when necessary, in order to prevent anticompetitive effects.

c) The licensing for the commercial or private use of spectrum (for broadcasting and telecommunication services), granted only through a public auction procedure run by IFT. The Institute publishes procedures for the respective public invitation to auction, on its website and in the Federal Official Gazette.

Source: Information provided by IFT, 2018.

Recommendations:

- ***Reassess*** if the functions and powers of the regulator are aligned with its roles and objectives, benchmarking internationally and taking into account evolution of sector. This exercise should in particular look at the division of responsibilities and functions between the regulator, the Ministry and Indecopi, and its aim should be to ensure a modernised role for the regulator to match current organisational, market and societal needs to effective regulate the telecommunications sector. Given its expertise, a more authoritative role on important decisions by the other public entities involved in the telecommunications sector should be considered. Given the dynamism of the sector, this assessment may need to be updated regularly.

- ***Continue*** monitoring trend of customer complaints and assess whether relevant regulation continues to contain loopholes that facilitate or allow for a gaming of the system in the area of complaints regarding billing. This assessment could make use of behavioural insights to consider why complaints have risen and how the issue could be resolved, based on an understanding of the actual behaviour of users and operators.

- ***Review*** approaches, functions and resources dedicated to consumer protection at the regulatory authority. This review should ensure that appropriate and proportional procedures are in place to carry out the consumer protection function of the regulator. This may include analysing if the regulator is over-stepping its role in committing resources to ensuring and monitoring user satisfaction and whether a more proportional attribution of resources could also be achieved through the roll out of more technology based engagement mechanisms.
- ***Evaluate*** the efficiency outcome of the two models of decentralised presence (regional offices and centres), and consider if cost-sharing arrangements could be extended also to offices. Outreach to users outside the Lima region should also increasingly build on digital and online tools and mechanisms.

Strategic planning

The regulator sets its strategic objectives in four-year Strategic Plans (*Plan Estratégico Institucional,* PEI) that have historically focused on competition, customer protection and organisational performance. These priorities are summarised in the regulator's mission statement: *to promote competition, quality of telecommunications services and user empowerment, in a continuous, efficient and timely manner*. The PEI is operationalised via a yearly work plan (*Plan Operacional Institucional*, POI). The current PEI 2018-2022 is structured into seven strategic institutional objectives (*Objetivos Estratégicos Institucionales*, OEIs) in two categories: four core objectives, pertaining to customer protection and competition functions, and three support objectives that relate to OSIPTEL corporate identity and organisational performance (Table 6). This is an evolution from the previous period that only counted with three objectives, one for each area (competition, user protection and organisational performance), and appears to put more emphasis on customer protection and satisfaction compared to the functioning of the market (three versus one core objective). The current plan was elaborated over a period of six months.

Recommendation:

- ***Share*** and build on OSIPTEL methodology defining its strategic framework and performance indicators with other public entities in Peru, while working on streamlining the indicators and decreasing burden of monitoring and reporting (See Section: Output and Outcome).

Communications

OSIPTEL has an active communications strategy that, while positive in terms of the reputation of the regulator, needs to be differentiated from formal stakeholder engagement channels. Peru's economic regulators have enjoyed visible public profiles since their creation. OSIPTEL counts with a strategic communications plan with differentiated activities for various target groups (for example, a newsletter that is directed at industry and congress, a blog for specialists and academics and personalised follow up for members of Congress). In 2016, the regulator invested in increasing their visibility in the media, resulting in a doubling of OSIPTEL media appearances from 2015 to 2016 (from 2 831 to 3 626). OSIPTEL is also very active on social media with over 84 000 followers on Twitter, 7 000 on LinkedIn, and 170 000 on Facebook. When coupled with more direct actions developed by OSIPTEL directly in municipalities in favour of engaging and informing users, the use of social media can significantly contribute to the regulator's strategic goal of empowering and informing consumers. Care should be taken to not substitute formal channels for stakeholder engagement and consultations, such as advisory or user councils, by exchanges and views on social media. When social media is being used to augment formal channels, it is important to make clear to the public how and why their comments are being considered versus engaging in unstructured exchanges about policy ideas. A variety of experiences and applications exist to support the use of social media for structured stakeholder engagement.

Box 4. Using social media for structured stakeholder engagement in Scotland

In Scotland, water and wastewater charges are reviewed and set every six years in a process called the Strategic Review of Charges that includes extensive stakeholder consultation. The purpose of the review is to ensure that Scottish Water, a publicly owned company, is adequately funded to deliver the objectives for the industry set by Scottish Ministers. For 2021-27 Review, the Water Industry Commission for Scotland (WICS), the water regulator in Scotland, is conducting the process in an innovative way by moving away from the traditional 'parent-child' relationship between the economic regulator and Scottish Water. Rather, WICS is building off the successful outcome from the previous 2015-21 Review where Scottish Water worked with a Consumer Forum, a body acting as a conduit for customer views, and other stakeholders to reach a settlement that reflects the views of customers and stakeholders, allowing the operator to take full ownership of its strategy and relationship with its customers.

As part of this innovative approach, the parties involved are using Behavioural Insights research, including working with Apptivism (a social purpose start-up that focuses on improving civic engagement with chat interfaces) to co-design a behaviourally-informed Facebook Messenger chatbot. Dubbed "ChatScotland," the bot solicited the public's views on water issues as a means of supporting the dialogue held in traditional customer engagement fora. ChatScotland received responses from 523 users over the 20 days of the pilot, providing feedback on participants' views, behaviours, knowledge and opinions on issues related to water. While ultimately the pilot was not chosen for use in future stages of the Review, it provided valuable lessons learned for leveraging social media for improved and structured stakeholder engagement.

Source: (Water Industry Commission for Scotland, 2017[3]); (Customer Forum,(n.d.)[4]); (Apptivism, 2018[5]).

Recommendation:

- ***Develop*** a holistic approach to bring together and clarify communications and official engagement mechanisms to extend the reach of OSIPTEL while making clear, separate, and consistent the appropriate avenues for information provision, complaints, claims, stakeholder engagement, and consultations. This approach should also take into account potential structured uses of social media as an additional means of stakeholder engagement.

Input

Financial resources and management

OSIPTEL is entirely funded by resources received from the regulated sector, but its budget is in practice limited by central government rules. The LMOR states that OSIPTEL's operational budget will be financed by income from the regulated industry up to 1% of operator income. In practice, this amount has been capped at 0.5% by the PCM since 2002, as per Supreme Decree 012-2002-PCM. Between 2015 and 2018 this amount declined by 19% in real terms as industry income decreased. This trend has led to the regulator feeling that its activities are under-funded and its resources are stretched too thin to carry out its regular activities. This feeling is exacerbated when new functions are added to OSIPTEL's portfolio in line with sector evolutions or new legislative texts (e.g. regulation of the National Fibre Optic Backbone). Table 4 shows execution of OSIPTEL budget for the period 2014-17, where it appears that budget execution is generally high and carry forward funds have on two occasions (2014 and 2017) provided funding for expenditure above the initial budget corresponding to the 0.5% fee on industry income.

Table 4. OSIPTEL annual budget and execution, 2014-18 (million PEN)

Year	2014	2015	2016	2017
Initial budget	79	96	82	81
Supplemental funds	24	8	12	12
Modified Institutional Budget (PIM)	103	104	94	93
Execution of initial budget (%)	120	85	94	107
Execution of Modified Institutional Budget (%)	92	79	82	93

Notes: Initial budget is sourced from funds collected from the regulatory contributions levied to regulated entities. Supplemental funds are approved by the MEF and added from the reserves of the regulator, arriving at the Modified Institutional Budget (PIM).
Source: Information provided by OSIPTEL, 2018.

Stronger evidence of a budget based on cost recovery of regulatory activities could strengthen the regulator's case for more resources and flexibility. As an autonomous regulator, OSIPTEL sends its budget proposal directly to the Ministry of Economy and Finance (*Ministerio de Economía y Finanzas*, MEF) for consideration in the national budget. The Peruvian national administration implements a performance-based budgeting system whereby budgets are to be aligned with goals and objectives of the institution and budget execution is monitored in parallel with progress in performance indicators. While the OSIPTEL budget is prepared with inputs from internal departments and compiled by the Planning and Budget Department (*Gerencia de Planeamiento y Presupuesto* GPP), the total amount of budget is set according to the available resources, rather than an estimation of the costs related to the regulation and supervision of the sector.

OSIPTEL is generally independent in managing its budget directly with MEF, although this is limited by a recent change in the use of carry-forward funds. OSIPTEL has historically been able to carry forward unspent funds, which has provided flexibility for handling emerging issues and fluctuations as seen above. The 2017 *Ley de Equilibrio Financiero,* renewed for 2018, required all public organisms to transfer unspent funds to the treasury, including those from directly collected resources (i.e. fines or fees), which were previously exempt from this rule. While OSIPTEL budget execution has generally been reasonably high, this new practice limits the autonomy of the regulator in managing its resources and directs income from regulated entities towards funding general government activities rather than those of the sector regulator.

Recommendations:

- ***Seek*** clarity on central administration constraints that impact on the regulator's funding model and financial management to better differentiate those linked to the current context on the one hand, and macro-economic policies on the other.
- ***Set up*** a practice whereby regulatory fees are reviewed every three years (or another regular and reasonable time frame) based on cost recovery principles of funding of economic regulators. Any unspent funds could be included in the calculation of the next regulatory fee, to lower the burden on industry over the next period. The review could also include benchmarking the appropriate level of the fee against other regulators.
- ***Engage*** in a systematic discussion with relevant stakeholders of additional resource needs generated by new functions or tasks assigned to the regulator when they arise. Given the dynamism of the sector, it is likely that these continue to grow and evolve over the next years. Transparently sharing analysis of the added draw on resources will constitute a good practice.
- ***Based*** on the principle of using income from industry to recover the costs of regulatory activities, advocate with other economic regulators for a review of the law regarding absorption of carry forward in regards the budget of economic regulators.

Box 5. Cost-recovery budgeting in Ireland and Canada

Ireland's Commission for Regulation of Utilities (CRU)

The CRU is funded entirely through levy and licence fees from relevant electricity, gas, petroleum safety, and water industry participants. Levies from market participants comprise the bulk of the CRU's income. The CRU sets its own budget without requiring government participation, and is defined annually on a cost-recovery basis in the fourth quarter of the year, on the basis of an estimate of CRU operating and capital budget required for the next year. There is no direct government contribution to the CRU budget and the regulator's annual budget is approved by the Commission without approval or *ex ante* assessment by the Oireachtas.

Annual budgets for the electricity, gas, petroleum and water are allocated by the CRU to each sector. Revenues, expenses and capital expenditure directly incurred by each sector are recorded in the separate budgets of the electricity, gas, petroleum and water sectors. Shared costs are allocated to each sector in proportion to the staff numbers engaged in the relevant sector. Costs linked to shared administrative functions such as finance, HR, IT, and Communications are pooled for all sectors.

Where annual expenditures exceed revenue, the balance is offset against the levy income for the subsequent year. The balances for the electricity, gas, petroleum and water sectors are recorded in their respective accounts, and audited on an annual basis by the Office of the Comptroller and Auditor General, which reports to the Public Accounts Committee of the Oireachtas. The CRU also conducts an annual internal audit, which is outsourced to an audit company).

Moreover, based on a risk assessment, a contingency fund is defined on a yearly basis to provide flexibility to deal with potential legal challenges or costs linked to safety cases or events. Any excess of revenue in the financial year is taken into account in determining the levy for the subsequent year per sector. The CRU can carry unspent funds over to the following year's budget without review or approval from external government entities.

National Energy Board of Canada (NEB)

Pursuant to the regulatory scheme in place, the Canadian NEB's cost recovery mechanism is premised on commodity charging costs that are allocated to specific entities within those sectors (oil – oil pipelines, gas – gas pipelines, etc.). Companies pay their share of recoverable costs to the Consolidated Revenue Fund of Canada, through greenfield levies, fixed levies (small, intermediate companies and other commodities) or proportional levies (large companies). The allocation of costs to commodity categories is based on time spent on each commodity.

The NEB also has an advisory committee, which is composed of the staff from the regulator and representatives of the regulated companies, that reviews planned expenditures and discusses cost recovery issues. The NEB does not receive this funding directly from companies; rather, it receives its appropriations through Parliament, on an annual basis.

Source: (OECD, 2018[6]); (OECD, 2016[7]).

Human resources and their management

The staff of OSIPTEL is recognised as highly technical and capable, but staff do not enjoy a uniform recruitment framework, limiting accountability. OSIPTEL employs 400 professionals who are mostly hired through open and transparent procedures based on a recruitment skills model, whereby the hiring manager makes a recommendation to the General Manager who makes the appointment. OSIPTEL also counts with six senior managers who are appointed under the *puestos de confianza* modality (General Manager, Administration and Finance Manager, Corporate Communications, Legal Advisor, Advisor to the President and Secretariat of the Board). These posts can be filled and dismissed at the discretion of the President of the Board without a competitive process. The President of the Board directly appoints the remaining senior management positions after a competitive recruitment process, who then serve on indeterminate contracts. The position of human resources manager is currently being created to further increase and improve HR management policies and practices.

Contracts, salaries and other benefits of OSIPTEL staff are governed by two different systems that may undermine staff motivation and HR practices. Peru's civil servants are currently regulated under one of three employment regimes, two of which are in use by regulatory authorities: a private activity regime that grants them indeterminate contracts and benefits such as health care (Law 728), and the Administrative Service Contracting (CAS) regime – a special temporary contracting regime with renewable 6-montsh contracts and some working benefits (Law 1057). The latter is meant to be a temporary contracting regime, but its use has grown beyond the intended temporary characteristic following the freezing of recruitments under Law 728, whereby new staff can only be hired under Law 728 in replacement of a departing staff member. As of 2018, OSIPTEL counts with 280 staff under Law 728 and 200 under Law 1057. The existence of two parallel frameworks may be problematic for accountability (hiring) and incentives for staff (remuneration, benefits). A new labour regime was created by SERVIR in 2013 as an administration-wide project seeks to create a unified employment regime for public officials including staff of economic regulators; but it is unclear when the SERVIR regime will be rolled out to Peru's regulatory authorities.

As many regulators worldwide, OSIPTEL struggles to attract and retain staff given the constraints of government employment frameworks, but it has implemented many successful initiatives to make OSIPTEL a desired place to work. In general salaries offered by OSIPTEL are somewhat higher than those offered by central government entities, but significantly below those of the private sector. To counter this challenge, the authority has developed a talent retention system that is central to its institutional identity as an employer. The plan includes a generous health insurance for the employee and their dependants, as well as training programmes. However, the former is only available to staff under Law 728 contracts. OSIPTEL also implements a robust performance assessment system, that since 2018 links staff objectives to the PEI, and includes also 360 degree evaluations of managers by staff. Thanks to all these efforts, OSIPTEL was in 2015 ranked as a Great Place to Work and boasts a turnover rate of only 9.13% compared to 18% across the Peruvian national administration (2017 figures). The authority also won the 2017 Premio Abe award for good labour practices in the category of best labour flexibility programme.

Recommendations:

- ***Seek*** to implement a human resource framework regarding diversity, recruitment, remuneration and incentives that takes into account the special needs of economic regulators to attract specialised innovative technical talent while competing with the private sector for available human resources.
- ***Level*** the playing field for staff between the different categories of contracts by advocating for the implementation of one unified system of contracts with similar benefits to support recruitment efforts.
- ***Share*** good practices and results in terms of talent retention and staff well-being across Peruvian national administration and other regulatory authorities.
- ***Consider*** the possibility of implementing transparent and open requirements and recruitments for all posts in the regulatory authority, in order to tap into as wide a pool of talent as possible, diversify teams and promote innovation by bringing in people with different experiences and perspectives. At least for more senior positions, this could include binding profiles with specific requirements in terms of degrees, level of experience and other characteristics such as language skills.

Process

Decision making

Decision making at OSIPTEL is led by the Board of Directors, which holds a wide mandate and is involved in a wide variety of executive decisions but seems to have little input at the strategic level. The Board is responsible for the administration and supervision of contracts and setting a clear mandate for the organisation. The Board exerts both normative and regulatory functions via resolutions, and issues technical opinions on concession contracts. The Board also designates and removes members of the appellate bodies (i.e. TRASU) that handle complaints and appeals presented to OSIPTEL, as well as acts as the appellate body for companies receiving sanctions levied by the Enforcement and Inspections department. This latter function is complicated by the lack of guidelines for Board members for ruling on cases, which may lead to variations in decisions over time. Given its limited resources, the Board seems to principally focus on executive decision making and not on providing strategic direction to OSIPTEL.

In its current configuration, the Board appears to operate under a hybrid model whereby its functions and resources are misaligned. The President of the Board holds a full-time executive position in the regulatory authority, while other Board members only serve on a part-time basis. They attend two board meetings per month and are remunerated only for these occasions, significantly limiting their capacity to weigh in on complex technical and strategic decisions. They take part in executive decision-making but have limited resources to support this participation that may be more reflective of an advisory role. While a limited number of advisors serve the President of the Board, they appear to only serve the President and do not support other members of the Board.

By design, members of the Board are appointed on staggered contracts for continuity in decision-making; in practice, this has not been followed, putting at risk stability and independence of the regulator. The Board is composed of five members, one of whom is its President. By law, all members are on staggered five-year terms that can be renewed once. In practice, however, the mandate of three out of five Board members expired in June 2018. Instead of appointing new members, Supreme Decree No. 082-2018-PCM issued by the PCM extended their mandates once by 90 days. At time of writing new members had yet to be appointed and the Board was operating with only two active members, including the President (see Table 5). This creates a risk for continuity and capacity to function of the Board. Board members are selected by a multi-step process with checks and balances that include review by an inter-institutional selection committee, submission of selected candidates to the President of the Republic by the President of the Council of Ministers, appointment by the President of the Republic by Supreme Decree, and finally endorsement the PCM, MEF and MTC. In the past 10 years, there have been no women on the OSIPTEL board.

Table 5. Ten-year history of OSIPTEL board members

Member	Role	Profession	Start date	End date
Rafael Eduardo Muente Schwartz	President	Lawyer	2017	2022
Jesús Eduardo Guillén Marroquín	Board member	Economist (PhD)	2017	2021
Manuel Ángel Cipriano Pirgo	Board member	Lawyer	2013	2018[1]
Jesús Otto Villanueva Napurí	Board member	Mechanical and electrical engineer	2013	2018[2]
Víctor Jesús Revilla Calvo	Board Member	Civil engineer	2015	2018[3]
Manuel Ángel Cipriano Pirgo	Board member	Lawyer	2013	2013[6]
Gonzalo Martín Ruiz Díaz	President	Economist (PhD)	2012	2017[4]
Humberto Eduardo Zolezzi Chacón	Board member	Electrical engineer	2011	2016[5]
Carlos Daniel Durand Chahud	Board member	Systems engineer	2010	2011
Víctor Jesús Revilla Calvo	Board member	Civil engineer	2010	2013[7]

Notes: 1., 2, & 3. Received 90 day extension according to Supreme Decree No. 072-2018-PCM; 4., 5., 6. & 7. stayed 60 calendar days after the end of their terms, in accordance with provisions in article 7 of the Regulations of the Framework Law, approved by Supreme Decree No. 042-2005-PCM.
Source: Information provided by OSIPTEL, 2018.

Box 6. Governing Board of Mexico's Federal Telecommunications Institute (IFT)

The 2013 reform of the Mexican constitution established the IFT as an autonomous, independent public agency with its own decision-making power and operations, with legal personality and its own assets. The authority was created for regulating spectrum, networks, services, competition and efficient development of the broadcasting and telecommunications sectors. It also acts as competition authority for these markets.

The Governing Board is the Institute's highest instance of governance and decision-making. It is composed of seven full-time Commissioners with voting rights, including its president. The IFT Chairman presides the Governing Board and Institute, and he is its legal representative.

The Commissioners remain in office for nine years. Their mandates are staggered to allow for continuity and are non-renewable. All commissioners have one vote, weigh in on complex decision-making in the sector and have non-delegable duties. All the Commissioners have to attend plenary sessions except for justifiable cause. Their powers are not limited and they are on an equal footing.

Source: information provided by IFT, 2018.

Recommendations:

- ***Assess*** whether the activity and duties of the Board reflect its mandate and structure. Consider ways to use limited available time to involve Board members in deciding on the long-term strategic direction of the organisation (including identifying priorities and targets) and monitoring the regulator's performance against this.
- ***Consider*** supporting informed decision making by the Board by making available advisory resources to all Board members, and proposing specialisation and responsibility for certain strategic areas that could rotate between members. These areas could correspond to technical areas or specific regulatory projects, rather than high level goals of the regulator. This would allow board members to focus on specific technical area and increase their level of responsibility and accountability.
- ***Remove*** any potential conflict of interest when reviewing the duties and structure of the Board.

Internal organisation and management

OSIPTEL is managed by the President of the Board, with the support of the General Manager. The General Manager is appointed at-will along with six members of the senior management of the organisation without open recruitment (*puestos de confianza*). The President approves the institutional budget, balance sheets and financial statements as well as the Institutional Management Plan and administrative policies. The General Manager is responsible for legal, administrative, and judicial responsibilities of OSIPTEL and plans, organises, manages, executes and supervises the administrative, operational, economic and financial activities of OSIPTEL. The General Manager also prepares draft annual reports, budgets and makes senior management recruitment decisions, which are approved by the President. The President is supported by two advisors, the General Manager by one. Together, the President and General Manager chair a weekly meeting with OSIPTEL senior management. A large number of decision making functions are concentrated in these two executive positions.

OSIPTEL seeks to reach excellence in terms of organisational processes and management. A high priority has been placed on obtaining international certifications for management and processes, including the SGSI Certification for ISO 27001 (information security management systems) and the SGS certification for ISO 9001 (quality management systems) in 2015. OSIPTEL has also been awarded a spot on the 2015 Great Places to Work list, the 2016 National Quality Award in the public sector category in recognition of its management model, and the 2017 Association of Good Employers (ABE) Award for Labour Social Responsibility in the category of Best Work Flexibility Program. Since 2003, a formal practice has existed to send preliminary analyses on draft regulations to the various internal departments for feedback via memo. In 2017, the General Manager improved this process by encouraging departments seeking feedback to provide concrete action points attached to the memo, including a timeline.

Recommendations:

- ***Review*** the internal governance and management processes to ensure adequate diversity in decision making between the President of the Board (strategic) and General Manager (management), including appropriate resources to carry out each function. A more spread out internal governance model with adequate delegation of authority and additional challenge functions could support a longer-term vision for the regulator, as well as promote stability in decision making.
- ***Introduce*** a deliberate mechanism for quality control and check that can also serve as a challenge function with regard to decision making and processes. Several options exist for these functions – for example, on the lighted side, explicit peer review mechanisms internally or externally, or, on the more structural side, by setting up a dedicated independent body in charge of this function. Reviews may need to take place at several stages in the process, rather only at the end, to provide meaningful opportunities to the scope and direction of the task or output.

Regulatory quality processes

OSIPTEL has been a pioneer in implementing regulatory quality assessments, along with other regulatory agencies and the PCM. In response to the 2016 *OECD Regulatory Review of Peru*, the PCM began developing a Regulatory Quality Assessment (RQA) framework that implements measures for simplifying administrative procedures, including a requirement to assess impacts as well as conduct stock reviews and *ex post* evaluations for regulations that add administrative processes. OSIPTEL, independently and in parallel, developed a manual and guidelines for applying Regulatory Impact Assessments (RIA) to all regulatory decisions and not just administrative processes. In 2017, OSIPTEL released a "regulatory quality commitment" to formalise goal of developing RIA and, in 2018, released the guidelines and manual for following PCM and internal requirements for RIA. While the guidelines and manual allow for multiple types analysis proportional to the issue at hand (including a full cost-benefit analysis), to date mainly multi-criteria analysis RIAs have been completed. All draft RIAs are overseen by the counsellor of the President of the Board, who is independent of the regulatory process and performs this quality assurance function in addition to their other duties. The counsellor has the power to block and send back inadequate RIAs before presenting to the Board.

Although not mandatory in Peru, stakeholder engagement is practiced consistently by OSIPTEL with internal and external stakeholders but only at the later stages of developing regulations. All regulators are required to publish new laws and regulations in the Official Gazette and on the institutional website for comments for at least 30 days. Comments received and actions taken in response are logged in a 'comments matrix' and published alongside the final regulation for transparency. Early-stage consultations are also occasionally conducted in an ad hoc manner when OSIPTEL requests information from regulated entities.

The further development of digital tools to support OSIPTEL regulatory activities could enhance engagement and quality of impact. While very active on social media, OSIPTEL mostly uses these resources as a means to share information to help consumers make better decisions. A mobile application is currently in development to allow users to report disruptions to their services. Exploring existing or new digital tools to enhance stakeholder engagement can help OSIPTEL reach a wider audience when conducting outreach and consulting or soliciting feedback from users and stakeholders.

There is no formal body dedicated to bringing together stakeholders for early stage consultation, limiting predictability and inclusivity of stakeholder engagement mechanisms. Regulated entities submit comments to OSIPTEL regulations through public consultations once regulatory proposals have been developed for a period of 30 days. Users are able to participate through the same mechanisms, but the user councils mandated by law have not been set up or operationalised by the regulator. The activation of the councils, built on adequate incentive mechanisms for them to engage in meaningful exchange, and their inclusion in more inclusive early stage consultation bodies could enhance the scope and usefulness of the regulator's stakeholder engagement activities.

***Ex post* reviews have not been consistently applied, but recent efforts have been undertaken to improve outdated and existing regulations.** In accordance with the PCM RQA, regulations adding administrative procedures must be reviewed every three years, with some exceptions. In OSIPTEL, most *ex post* evaluations are conducted ad hoc or only for specific regulations. Some regulations, often involving prices or interconnection charges, are reviewed on a regular basis, based on a sunset clause or through existing norms. There is no formal guideline for *ex post* evaluations, including in terms of engaging stakeholders. Each department is responsible for reviewing its respective regulations through established criteria. In accordance with the RQA guidelines, OSIPTEL is currently reviewing its stock of regulations. While the RQA requires focuses on administrative processes, OSIPTEL is extending this review to their entire stock of regulations issued since its creation. It aims to review four regulations in 2018 and complete the entire process by 2021. An external consultant has been engaged to provide a diagnostic on burdensome regulations for businesses and an ad hoc group has been created to conduct the process. This group will deliver its conclusions in 2019. From 2019 to 2021, OSIPTEL will repeal, modify, or leave unchanged the regulations in accordance with the recommendations.

Box 7. Ofcom's Communications Consumer Panel (CCP)

The Communications Act 2003 requires Ofcom – the telecommunications regulator in the United Kingdom – to set up and maintain effective arrangements for consultation with consumers. These arrangements include the establishment of the Communications Consumer Panel, an independent body with the function of advising both Ofcom and other government entities.

The Panel consists of eight experts who work to protect and promote people's interests in the communications sector by carrying out research, providing advice and encouraging Ofcom, the Government, the EU, industry and others to look at issues through the eyes of consumers, citizens and small businesses. Four members of the Panel represent the interests of consumers in England, Northern Ireland, Scotland and Wales respectively.

The CPP is mandated to meet at least 11 times per year, with quorum set at 4 members plus the Chairperson with provisions that allow for attendance through telephone or video link for the purposes of determining a quorum. Formal minutes are taken and, once approved, posted on the CPP website as well as submitted directly to the Ofcom Board. The Panel is provided a budget for members' remuneration, expenses, and to commission work. For the 2015-16 fiscal year, this was GBP 370 000, of which GBP 240 000 went to support functions (including an Advisory Team, research, consultancy, stakeholder relations, and design and publication).

The Panel pays particular attention to the needs of vulnerable people; older people; people with disabilities; and micro businesses. Cross-membership with Ofcom's Advisory Committee on Older and Disabled People (ACOD) was established in 2012. Members, in their ACOD capacity, also provide advice to Ofcom on issues relating to older and disabled people which includes content on television, radio and other services regulated by Ofcom.

Source: Information provided by Ofcom: https://www.ofcom.org.uk/about-ofcom/how-ofcom-is-run/committees/communications-consumer-panel and https://www.communicationsconsumerpanel.org.uk/, 2018.

Recommendations:

- ***Maintain*** momentum towards the full implementation of the new RIA system, including the application of various methods according to the principle of proportionality.
- ***Review*** and make necessary changes to activate the users' council mandated by law to provide structured engagement with users of telecommunications services as well as an avenue for early and open consultation.
- ***Create*** an advisory committee of stakeholders for transparent and early consultation with industry, users, and other relevant stakeholders as a means to enhance the inclusiveness and predictability of OSIPTEL regulatory activities. In setting up the council, care will need to be taken to ensure adequate balance between participants and perspectives.

- ***Develop*** use of digital tools for regulatory activities, including building bespoke tools for specific sectoral needs (i.e. the mobile application currently in development) but also using existing tools such as WhatsApp and Twitter for more structured and effective consultation and feedback.
- ***Develop*** and disseminate an annual regulatory programme that would present the regulator's activities with regard to the development of new regulations and would contribute to minimising short-term activities.
- ***Use*** the lessons learned from evaluating the entire stock of regulations to extend *ex post* evaluations as a consistent and automatic component of policy making at OSIPTEL.

Box 8. Institutionalising stakeholder participation: Mexico's energy regulators

Mexico's Energy Regulatory Commission (*Comisión Reguladora de Energía*, CRE) has established two advisory bodies – one for hydrocarbons and one for electricity – with the purpose of discussing CRE's regulatory plans (in addition to specific regulations that will be submitted to public consultation).

These advisory bodies were constituted by representatives of different stakeholders: investors, utilities, consumers, government and academia. Following the introduction of an energy reform in 2013, CRE will replace these two bodies with an "Advisory Board", a body that is formally established in the commission statutes.

Mexico's National Hydrocarbons Commission (*Comisión Nacional de Hidrocarburos*, CNH) includes a public consultation procedure in the drafting of regulations that comprises the installation of advisory councils proposed by the Governing Council of the CNH. The Advisory Council is a forum whose purpose is to contribute to the public consultation process through the opinions of the interested sectors and thus to improve the content of the regulation.

For the elaboration of the technical provisions for the use of associated natural gas in the exploration and extraction of hydrocarbons (issued by the CNH and published in the Official Gazette 7 January 2016) an Advisory Council was created with representatives of leading institutions in the energy and academic sectors, and associations that group assignees and contractors, among others, in order to discuss the preliminary draft.

Representatives of energy sector institutions including ASEA, the Under Secretariat of Hydrocarbons of the Ministry of Energy and the Mexican Petroleum Institute, the Mexican Association of Hydrocarbons Companies (AMEXHI), the Mexican Union of Engineers Associations, and the Confederation of Employers of the Mexican Republic (COPARMEX) participated. Regarding the academic sector, the National Autonomous University of Mexico (UNAM), the National Polytechnic Institute (IPN), the National Council of Science and Technology (CONACYT), the College of Engineers of Mexico and the Mario Molina Center participated.

Two sessions were held: the first on 19 June 2015 and the second on 1 September 2015. In the first meeting, representatives of the CNH explained the purpose and the criteria of the regulation. Participants analysed the draft and sent comments 30 June 2015. The CNH analysed them and compiled a list with all the comments. At this stage the CNH received 133 observations divided into 96 opinions of a legal nature, and 37 of a technical nature.

During the second meeting, representatives of the CNH informed the participants how their comments were received, as well as the reasons for those that were not received.

In this way, the Advisory Council allows for CNH to know and take into account the opinion of sectors interested in the regulation, to strengthen the technical aspects and to strengthen the process of transparency in the issuance of regulations.

Source: Information provided by CRE, October 2014; Information provided by CNH (March 2017).

Inspection and enforcement

Inspection plans are made yearly and seek to visit new areas each year, but are not informed by a risk-based strategy. The Enforcement and Supervision Department (*Gerencia de Supervisión y Fiscalización*, GSF) is equipped with professional staff in Lima as well as 1 inspector in each of the 23 decentralised offices who transmit information to Lima. Inspectors are specialised in different areas – including engineering, law and economics – to ensure a multi-disciplinary approach. Supervisions are conducted with the goal of compliance and prevention. In 2016 and 2017, OSIPTEL conducted 260 and 250 inspections, respectively with 126 and 99 cases of non-compliance detected. Administrative sanctioning is the most common result, but OSIPTEL also uses corrective or preventative actions in order to give regulated entities various opportunities to correct behaviour.

Sanctions involve a lengthy administrative procedure and their level is set by the General Manager. The governing regulation gives the procedure and ranges for sanctions (according to three levels: light, moderate or heavy), which are normally in accordance with economic principles. The line department forwards a proposal to the General Manager who can approve or revise the sanction to increase or decrease the amount within the bounds of the governing regulation. The regulated entity can appeal the sanction to the Board of Directors. All sanctions are published on website as part of the mandatory procedure. OSIPTEL wants to extend this provision and publish all decisions to include the case of no sanction.

Recommendations:

- ***Adopt*** a risk-based strategy to inspections and enforcement and review methods for streamlining the sanctioning process to achieve desired behaviour changes faster and more efficiently, for the benefit of consumers, in line with the OECD Best Practice Principles and the OECD Toolkit on Enforcement and Inspections.
- ***Assess*** the validity and accountability of decision making in setting the level of sanctions as well as reviewing appeals in first instance, in the interest of transparency and stability in the process.

Transparency, integrity and accountability

OSIPTEL places a high priority on transparent and accountable decisions making. OSIPTEL is committed to publishing all regulatory, supervisory, and normative decisions on its website supported by the raw datasets and other relevant non-confidential information used to render their decisions. It makes available raw data collected from industry on its website, and uses this data to produce easy-to-read regular reports on the telecommunications sector using data collected from industry, as well as a number of newsletters, videos, and statistical reports. It also publishes information on its activities, such as meetings and a list of people met. Information distribution is supported by a well-developed communications strategy directed towards Congress, executive bodies, industry, users, and the media.

While OSIPTEL shares information on sector performance and its activities via multiple outreach products, formal accountability mechanisms are lacking. On the one hand, OSIPTEL develops a number of tools to communicate on its activities, the efficiency of which may be increased by streamlining. On the other hand, the regulator is not required to present or discuss its annual report with Congress. While OSIPTEL can be called to appear before the Congress and its committees, the annual reports of OSIPTEL are not scrutinised on a regular basis. More structured reporting can serve the dual role of contributing to a "no surprises" relationship with the legislative branch as well as increasing understanding of the regulator's work by Congresspersons.

Peru's economic regulators including OSIPTEL should seek to be exemplary in the areas of integrity and transparency, given their role in providing stability to the sectors they oversee. OSIPTEL has an Institutional Code of Ethics displayed prominently throughout the workplace and an ethics working group with representatives from each department responsible for promoting ethical behaviour. The Ethics Code includes five fairly general dispositions and does not lay out supervisory and enforcement mechanisms, although violations to the Code of Ethics are subject to sanctions and reported to a designated person (currently the Advisor to the President of the Board). This person accepts responsibility on top of their regular work duties. Violations are handled by an ethics committee, with severe violations escalated to the Human Resources Manager and the SERVIR tribunal in the most severe cases. Violations are not reported anonymously and, to date, none have been reported.

OSIPTEL operates an 'open-door' policy for regulated entities to discuss issues with the regulator, with recent changes barring this from occurring during the regulatory development phase. Entities then have to wait until public consultation to provide their inputs into draft laws. Previously, entities would speak directly with Board members and with regulator staff, with record of the visit in the online Transparency Portal (name of entity and representatives visiting, headline about the topic discussed, and OSIPTEL staff met) but not a detailed description of what was discussed.

Recommendations:

- ***Put*** in place a regular engagement activity with the Congress to increase accountability as well as understanding of the regulator's role and activities by the legislature. This could, for example, take place once a year as a reporting on performance and results around the regulator's annual report.
- ***Assess*** the impact of the various reporting and transparency tools currently implemented by OSIPTEL and potentially, streamline.
- ***Strengthen*** mechanisms to supervise and enforce OSIPTEL Code of Ethics with the goal of creating a culture of integrity, transparency and justice that provides channels for protected disclosure for whistle blowers and adequate methods for handling complaints in line with the OECD Recommendation on Public Integrity.
- ***Further*** refine the online transparency portal to provide full information about visits by regulated entities and other groups, as well as further communicate on the existence of this tool and guidance for staff on how to deal with these meetings to promote a constructive dialogue with industry. Improving the oversight mechanism and formalising rules can be introduced to promote

transparency and minimise conflict of interest, while providing an avenue for constructive suggestions on regulations before becoming draft texts.

- ***Consider*** live streaming meetings of the Board for full transparency in decision making, when feasible from a confidentiality point of view.

Output and outcome

Performance assessment

OSIPTEL's strategic framework includes a mix of outcome and organisational goals, and is supported by sophisticated indicators to measure their achievement. The Strategic framework is composed of seven strategic objectives, with three focusing on consumer protection, one on competition, and three on OSIPTEL reputation and processes. The strategic institutional objectives (OEIs) are measured by high-level indicators that mostly focus on market outcomes, but targets are not fixed for them for the strategic planning period (see Table 6). These OEIs are then translated into priority actions that count with their batch of indicators, mostly focused on outputs, processes, and inputs. Furthermore, OSIPTEL has designed composite indicators (indices) that measure market performance for the OEIs and further (for example, the competition index that brings together all areas under OSIPTEL purview). OSIPTEL also shares data to inform a set of indicators defined by MEF for monitoring budget execution and performance. Not all MEF indicators are included in the overall strategic framework of the regulator which can lead to a duplication of efforts in terms of monitoring.

Table 6. OSIPTEL strategic objectives and indicators, 2018-2022

TYPE	STRATEGIC OBJECTIVE	INDICATOR
CORE	Promote competition between telecommunications operators	• Mobile telephony competition index • Mobile telephony price index • Mobile internet competition index • Mobile internet price index • Fixed internet competition index • Fixed internet price index • Pay TV competition index • Pay TV price index
	Guarantee compliance with quality standards in telecommunications services, as established or offered by the operators	• Mobile telephony quality of service index • Mobile internet quality of service index • Fixed internet quality of service index • Pay TV quality of service index
	Promote appropriate attention to users by operators	• % of compliance with quality of service standards in customer service by operators • % of user satisfaction with quality of customer service by operator
	Empower telecommunications service users	• % of users who know they basic rights • % of users with problems with service who found an adequate solution
SUPPORT	Consolidate OSIPTEL's reputation as a transparent and highly specialised institution	• OSIPTEL reputation index
	Consolidate the management model of OSIPTEL towards excellence	• % of internal client satisfaction with Line bodies • % of internal client satisfaction with Support and Advisory bodies • OSIPTEL management excellency index
	Implement processes for disaster risk management	• Number of implementation or update reports for disaster risk management

Source: (OSIPTEL, 2018[1]).

Sophisticated indicators exist to measure the achievement and implementation of the PEI, but their monitoring may be very resource intensive and under-utilised for accountability and transparency purposes. OSIPTEL has defined 14 composite indicators that measure the achievement of four of the OEIs, the others being monitored by satisfaction percentages or number of reports. However, OSIPTEL is not required to report on these indicators to Congress or other bodies, and while a sophisticated annual report is prepared, the indicators are used mostly for internal purposes. Moreover, OSIPTEL is only required to report on a sub-set of their total indicators to MEF and PCM, who also request different sub-sets themselves. The lack of alignment between indicators and reporting requirements could reduce the efficiency of the accountability and transparency systems towards improving the performance of the regulator.

Recommendations:

- ***Share*** the good experience of OSIPTEL strategic framework with other economic regulators and other Peruvian public bodies.
- ***Streamline*** PEI and POI indicators for more focused efforts and resources on monitoring and reporting. The aim of the indicators would be to support the management of the regulator and decisions on strategic (re)orientation.
- ***Explore*** including targets for indicators in the strategic framework and monitor achievement of these targets in reporting.

Data and reporting

OSIPTEL requests a number of data and information from regulated entities and publishes and uses the data through varied channels. Regulated companies are required to submit 185 forms via an online digitised system, as well as to respond to punctual requests for information sent by OSIPTEL. When incomplete or inconsistent information is sent, OSIPTEL issues letters requesting the operator to comply. Regulated entities can furthermore receive sanctions for non- or late-compliance with reporting requirements. It is also difficult for OSIPTEL to adequately use all this data in reports or communications materials, which may lead to resentment from industry. OSIPTEL is developing methods for using more of the data it collects, but also should evaluate whether or not it is collecting too much data in the first place. Most data that is not confidential is available in raw format on the OSIPTEL website. OSIPTEL reports on the performance of the sector in its annual report, as well as through snapshots in its quarterly newsletter and brief statistical reports. However, the regulator does not publish a dedicated and systematic report on the performance of the sector nor does it use the existing channels as opportunities to engage with regulated entities on market trends and evolutions.

The varied reports published by the regulator could be streamlined into more targeted and integrated reporting in line with the regulator's strategic framework. The regulator collects a large amount of data to inform its performance indicators and publishes analysis and some raw data. Among the information that is published online are raw market data, raw data from consumer survey, analysis of consumer survey, brief statistical reports that present market trends and performance, working papers. OSIPTEL also communicates on its activities and impact via regular newsletters and produces a detailed annual report. The only obligatory reporting is to MEF on a set of indicators agreed with the Ministry, which does not necessarily coincide with OSIPTEL's own set of indicators within its strategic framework. The strategic framework and review of indicators, as well as publication of all OSIPTEL communication outputs is resource intensive.

Recommendations:

- ***Further*** align the annual report to the strategic framework and use it as an opportunity to communicate on achievement against the strategic objectives.
- ***Review*** the scope of market performance snapshots prepared by OSIPTEL in favour of a predictable annual market performance report, which could be used as an opportunity to engage with industry. This report would be different from the general institutional annual report.
- ***Review*** the current data collection policies to ensure it is still fit for purpose and appropriate for achieving the strategic goals of the regulator to limit the data compliance burden on industry, with a priority given to only collecting data that can be reasonably used by the regulator.
- ***Organise*** public event with stakeholders for the presentation of the annual report.
- ***Explore*** opportunity to streamline or reduce data reporting requirements to alleviate issues relating to inconsistency and incomplete information, particularly by reviewing the processes through which data is collected e.g. the forms, how data is asked and understood, how easy/complicated is the data collection process.

Box 9. Sector engagement and reporting: the PSA (Norway) and Ofcom (UK)

Norway's Petroleum Safety Agency (PSA)

The PSA developed the Trend in Risk Level Project (RNNP) in 1999 as a consensual measurement tool of the level of risk in Norway's offshore petroleum sector, in response to disagreements on the level of risk between different parties. Since its conception, the RNNP has become an essential yearly activity of PSA.

A key output is the identification of relevant indicators that reflect different aspects of risk relevant to the petroleum industry. The RNNP relies on close collaboration with other parties, including on feedback from the industry on methodology and indicators, to guarantee agreement on a reliable description of the level of risk. Industry participation in the early stages of the process is also essential to ensure the collection of good quality data for the exercise. The project is supported by highly qualified safety experts from national academic institutions, industry, and other specialists.

Engagement with stakeholders as well as the publication of the RNNP annual report take place within the Safety Forum, established in 2001 to initiate, discuss and follow up relevant safety, emergency preparedness and working environment issues in the petroleum industry, both offshore and at land facilities, in a tripartite perspective. The forum is led by the Director-general of PSA and brings together industry associations and trade unions.

The output of the RNNP is an annual report at industry level (no results on identifiable companies are published), which is presented in the Safety Forum. The presentation identifies areas for improvement and challenges the industry to identify corrective measures and to implement them. In addition to this direct impact on industry actions to mitigate risk, the exercise also helps PSA identify strategic priorities and plan its supervisory activities.

United Kingdom's telecommunications regulator: Ofcom

Ofcom publishes an annual Communications Market Report (CMR), which provides statistics and analysis on the UK communications sector as a reference for industry, stakeholders, academics and consumers. It also provides context to the work Ofcom undertakes in furthering the interests of consumers and citizens in the markets they regulate. The report contains data and analysis on broadcast television and radio, fixed and mobile telephony, internet take-up and consumption, and post.

The report is published in three formats: an interactive report that can be explored and customised in great depth, the narrative report that supplements the interactive report, and a summary of key statistics. Data is made available to download.

Ofcom publishes this report to support their regulatory goal to research markets constantly and to remain at the forefront of technological understanding. It also fulfils the requirements on Ofcom under Section 358 of the Communications Act 2003 to publish an annual factual and statistical report, as well as to undertake and make public their consumer research, as set out in Sections 14 and 15 of the Communications Act.

The CMR is published in August to ensure that it attracts a certain amount of attention, and care is taken to not publish any other document at this time.

Source: (Lauridsen, 2012[8]), *Trends in Risk Level Norwegian Petroleum Activity (RNNP)*, www.ptil.no/trends-in-risk-level/category155.html (accessed 2 November 2018); (Ofcom, 2018[9]), *The Communications Market 2018*, https://www.ofcom.org.uk/research-and-data/multi-sector-research/cmr/cmr-2018 (accessed 2 November 2018).

References

ACCC (2018), *Compliance & enforcement policy & priorities*, https://www.accc.gov.au/about-us/australian-competition-consumer-commission/compliance-enforcement-policy-priorities#about-this-policy (accessed on 02 November 2018). [2]

Apptivism (2018), *ChatScotland*, http://www.apptivism.org/ChatScotland (accessed on 10 January 2019). [5]

Customer Forum((n.d.)), *Customer Forum - About Us*, https://www.customerforum.org.uk/about-us/ (accessed on 10 January 2019). [4]

Lauridsen, Ø. (2012), *Trends in Risk Level Norwegian Petroleum Activity (RNNP)*, http://www.ptil.no/trends-in-risk-level/category155.html (accessed on 02 November 2018). [8]

OECD (2018), *Driving Performance at Ireland's Commission for Regulation of Utilities*, The Governance of Regulators, OECD Publishing, Paris, http://dx.doi.org/10.1787/9789264190061-en. [6]

OECD (2016), *Being an Independent Regulator*, The Governance of Regulators, OECD Publishing, Paris, http://dx.doi.org/10.1787/9789264255401-en. [7]

Ofcom (2018), *The Communications Market 2018*, https://www.ofcom.org.uk/research-and-data/multi-sector-research/cmr/cmr-2018 (accessed on 02 November 2018). [9]

OSIPTEL (2018), *Plan Estratégico Institucional 2018-22*, OSIPTEL, https://www.osiptel.gob.pe/repositorioaps/data/1/1/1/PAR/res025-2018-pd/Res025-2018-PD_PEI2018-2022.pdf (accessed on 22 June 2018). [1]

Water Industry Commission for Scotland (2017), *Innovation and Collaboration: future proofing the water industry for customers*, Water Industry Commission for Scotland (WICS), https://www.watercommission.co.uk/UserFiles/Documents/SRC21_Innovation%20and%20Collaboration_Methodology_WICS_amended.pdf (accessed on 10 January 2019). [3]

Chapter 1. Regulatory and sector context

This chapter describes the main features of the sectors regulated by Peru's telecommunications regulator (Organismo Supervisor de Inversión Privada en Telecomunicaciones, OSIPTEL). It also provides an overview of Peru's public institutions, and institutional and regulatory reforms.

Institutions

Peru has a centralised system of government which is comprised of the executive, legislative and judiciary branches.

Executive

The President of the Republic, the Council of Ministers, and the Presidency of the Council of Ministers (*Presidencia del Consejo de Ministros*, PCM) constitute the core bodies of the executive branch (see Figure 1.1, (OECD, 2016[1]). Along with the PCM, the Ministry of Economy and Finance (*Ministerio de* Economía *y Finanzas*, MEF) and the Ministry of Justice and Human Rights (*Ministerio de Justicia y Derechos Humanos,* MINJUS) help shape the overall regulatory environment in Peru. In the telecommunications sector, the Ministry of Transport and Communications (*Ministerio de Tranporte y Comunicaciones*, MTC) and other public bodies, such as the National Institute for the Defense of Competition and Intellectual Property (*Instituto Nacional de Defensa de la Competencia y Protección de la Propiedad Intelectual*, Indecopi), also work closely with OSIPTEL to improve regulatory policy in the sector.

Figure 1.1. Structure of the executive branch of the Peruvian government

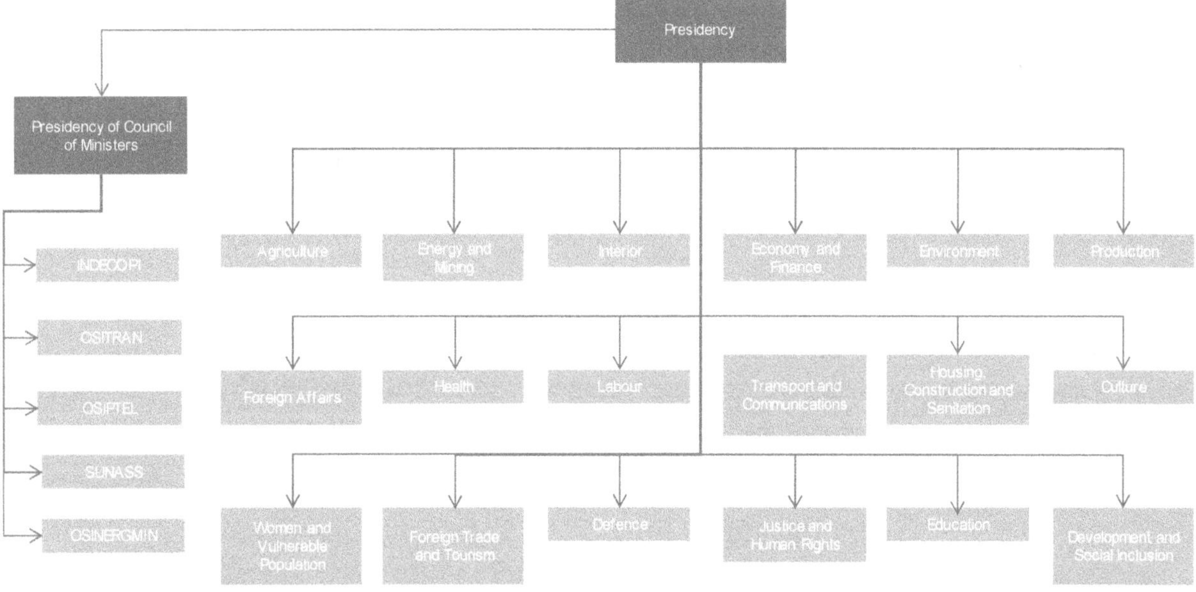

Note: The PCM also houses a large number of public entities, secretariats and commissions, which are not included in this figure.
Source: (OECD, 2016[2]), *Regulatory Policy in Peru: Assembling the Framework for Regulatory Quality*, OECD Reviews of Regulatory Reform, OECD Publishing, Paris, http://dx.doi.org/10.1787/9789264260054-en.

Presidency of the Council of Ministers (PCM)

The Presidency of the Council of Ministers (PCM) is responsible for co-ordinating national and sector policies within the executive, including line Ministries and public agencies. The PCM houses several secretariats and commissions, and manages and co-ordinates line ministries and public entities, as defined by law. The PCM oversees and provides guidance on the general administrative processes within OSIPTEL and plays a key role in appointing and nominating the President and the members of the Board of the regulator, as well as administering budget allocations and disbursements. The PCM is currently developing guidelines and functions to strengthen its regulatory oversight role in the Peruvian administration. While not formally defined in law, the President of the Council of Ministers in practice plays the role of Prime Minister and government spokesperson (OECD, 2016[1]).

The PCM houses several public entities, secretariats and commissions. Of these, OSIPTEL mainly interacts with two entities: the National Centre for Strategic Planning (*Centro Nacional de Planeamiento estratégico,* CEPLAN) and National Civil Service Authority (*Autoridad Nacional del Servicio Civil,* SERVIR):

- CEPLAN is a specialised technical body that is responsible for overseeing the national development plan as well as ensuring that sectoral, strategic, and operational plans of concerned government bodies are developed according to the National System of Strategic Planning (SINAPLAN, see Box 1.1). CEPLAN also monitors compliance and ensures that objectives and indicators set by the executive body are not contradictory with other sectoral or national plans.
- SERVIR sets human resources policies for the Peruvian public sector,[1] including OSIPTEL. It is responsible for orienting, monitoring, and managing human resource development, such as those relating to performance evaluations, information systems, remuneration, incentives and codes of conduct. Under the new SERVIR employment regime (see Box 2.2) the Body of Public Managers (Cuerpo de Gerentes Públicos, CGP) will be also responsible for carrying out the selection process for managerial positions. Under the new SERVIR 412 public entities have started the implementation of the new regime; however, as of 2018, no public entity has fully implemented the regime. Therefore, SERVIR has not selected managerial positions at OSIPTEL so far.

Box 1.1. Peru's National Strategic Development Plan (PEDN) and the National System of Strategic Planning (SINAPLAN)

In 2011, the government developed the National Strategic Development Plan (*Plan Estratégico de Desarrollo Nacional*, PEDN), which sets the strategic objective, policy guidelines, goals, and projects of the government for the next ten years. The plan consists of six strategic axes: "i) fundamental rights and dignity of persons; ii) opportunities and access to services; iii) state and governability; iv) economy, competitiveness, and employment; v) regional development and infrastructure; and vi) natural resources and environment" (CEPLAN, 2018[3]). The plan serves as guidance rather than a long-term action plan and provides flexibility in meeting goals in the medium-term by establishing annual goals every five years. The national plan was last updated in October 2015 and entitled as to include scenarios and targets for the country by 2021 (CEPLAN, 2018[4]).

The PEDN therefore serves as the National Centre for Strategic Planning's (CEPLAN) guidance for the application of the National System of Strategic Planning (*Sistema Nacional de Planeamiento Estratégico*, SINAPLAN). SINAPLAN is an articulated set of systems and co-ordination mechanisms to assure the viability of and co-operation in the national planning process and promote sustained development in the country (CEPLAN, 2018[4]).

Entities that make up the SINAPLAN include the three branches of government (executive, legislative, and judicial), autonomous constitutional organisations, sub-national governments, and the national forum that includes political parties and civil society organisations.

Source: (CEPLAN, 2018[3]), *Politicas y Planes*, http://www.ceplan.gob.pe/politicas-y-planes/ (accessed on 22 June 2018); (CEPLAN, 2018[4]), *Qué es el Sinaplan?*, http://www.ceplan.gob.pe/sinaplan/ (accessed on 22 June 2018); (OECD, 2016[5]), *Multi-dimensional Review of Peru: Volume 2. In-depth Analysis and Recommendations*, OECD Development Pathways, OECD Publishing, Paris, http://dx.doi.org/10.1787/9789264264670-en.

Ministry of Economy and Finance (MEF)

The Ministry of Economy and Finance (MEF) is responsible for the development of economic and financial policy in the country and plays an equally important role in regulatory quality efforts. MEF manages the performance-based budgeting system, which apply to all executive bodies and economic regulators, as well as other activities on regulatory policy related to administrative simplification, international regulatory co-operation, inter-governmental co-ordination, performance-based regulation, *ex ante* impact assessments of regulation, and governmental transparency and consultation. It has the capacity to assess draft policies with potential impact on commerce and other cross-cutting issues (OECD, 2016[2]).

The *ex ante* and *ex post* impact assessments began in 2010 under the leadership of the General Directorate of Public Budget (*Dirección General de Presupuesto Público*) of MEF, which directs, participates and supervises each of the stages of the evaluation process. Evaluated interventions can be activities, projects, programs or policies in progress or completed. To date, impact evaluations of public interventions of various sectors such as Education, Agriculture, Social Inclusion, Work, Citizen Security and Health have been developed.[2] In parallel, the Subsecretariat for Simplification and Regulatory Analysis (Subsecretaría de Simplificación y Análisis Regulatorio) implements methodologies and actions for Regulatory Impact Analysis (RIA) in the regulatory training process, in its areas of competence. It also issues opinions and advises public entities on the adequacy of the regulatory impact analysis in the regulatory training process (article 45 Regulation of Organization and Functions of the PCM, Supreme Decree 22-2017-PCM).

Attached to MEF is the Agency for the Promotion of Investment (*Agencia de Promoción de la Inversión Privada,* ProInversión), which is a specialised technical body responsible for the promotion of national investments through public-private partnerships (PPPs) in services, infrastructure, assets, and other state projects. It also responsible for providing information and orientation services to investors, mediating different views on investment projects, and creating a conducive environment for attracting private investments, in accordance with economic plans and integration policies, such as those related to the development of telecommunications infrastructure. ProInversión receives technical comments from OSIPTEL, MEF and the MTC when developing investment projects; however, only MEF and the MTC opinions are considered binding.

Ministry of Justice (MINJUS)

MINJUS acts as a legal advisory body for the executive branch. It has a broad mandate to improve the quality of the rule of law and act as a legal quality check for draft regulations. Together with the PCM and MEF, it is considered among the most influential ministries in the executive branch. MINJUS ensures that the executive branch performs its duties within the political constitution of Peru by providing legal advice and opinions on regulatory initiatives. It is also the agency within the executive branch responsible for co-ordinating with the judicial branch, the public prosecutor, and related entities within the judicial system.

Ministry of Transport and Communications (MTC)

The Ministry of Transport and Communications (MTC) is responsible for defining and developing policies for Peru's transportation systems and telecommunications sector. It is in charge of designing, leading, promoting, and implementing actions aimed at providing efficient transportation and telecommunication systems and overseeing concession programmes within its sectors. This is done in conjunction with control bodies and sectoral institutions that supervise the proper operation of telecommunications and transport activities, namely two of the country's four economic regulators: OSIPTEL and OSITRAN.

The MTC establishes the general policy and direction of the telecommunications sector and oversees the implementation of various projects, such as those undertaken through the Telecommunications Investment Fund (*Fondo de Inversión en Telecomunicaciones*, FITEL). The MTC is responsible for assessing, processing, and supervising requests related to the operation of open-signal radio, radio spectrum, and television stations and the provision of private telecommunications services.

Independent regulatory bodies

Regulatory authorities

Peru created four economic regulators in the 1990s as part of a broader policy built on the pillars of economic liberalisation, private investment attraction and regulated competition. These authorities exist today under the following names: the Supervisory Agency for Private Investment in Telecommunications (*Organismo Suupervisor de Inversión Privada en Telecomunicaciones,* OSIPTEL), the Supervisory Agency for Investment in Energy and Mining (*Organismo Supervisor de la Inversión en Energía y Minería,* OSINERGMIN),[3] the Supervisory Agency for Investment in Public Transport Infrastructure (*Organismo Supervisor de la Inversión en Infraestructura de Transporte de Uso Público,* OSITRAN), and the National Superintendence of Sanitation Services (*Superintendencia Nacional de Servicios de Saneamiento,* SUNASS).[4] They were created to foster competition and promote infrastructure investment following the liberalisation of the economy. The defining features of these entities are: 1) institutional design as administratively independent bodies of the central government; 2) funding scheme through industry contributions; and 3) collegiate decision-making body.

Competition and consumer protection authority

In addition to the four economic regulators, the National Institute for the Defense of Free Competition and the Protection of Intellectual Property (*Instituto Nacional de Defensa de la Competencia y de la Protección de la Propiedad Intelectual,* Indecopi)[5] was created in

1992 as an independent regulatory body in charge of enforcing competition law and intellectual property law.[6] Since 2010, Indecopi is also responsible for protecting consumers across the economy as the National Consumer Protection Authority, exercising its duties within the framework of the National Consumer Protection and Defense Policy, and based on four strategic pillars: 1) education, orientation, and dissemination; 2) protection of consumer health and safety; 3) mechanisms for the prevention and solution of conflicts between providers and consumers; and 4) strengthening of the National Integrated Consumer Protection System.

It has the authority to make binding decisions over sanctions or penalties for violations in accordance with Law 29571, Code for the Protection and Defense of the Consumer (*Código de Protección y Defensa del Consumidor*). Penalties are capped at 50 tax units (PEN 207 500) for minor infractions, 150 tax units (PEN 622 500) for serious infractions and 450 tax units (PEN 1.9 million) for very serious infractions.[7]

Since 2013, Indecopi has been conducting *ex post* reviews of regulations within their jurisdiction and has eliminated nearly 3 000 regulations in the country. Importantly, in the telecommunications sector, competition functions are retained by the economic sector regulator rather than Indecopi, except for unfair competition related to advertising. With regard to consumer protection, Indecopi is responsible for hardware-related issues whereas, OSIPTEL, which also has consumer protection functions within the telecommunications market, is responsible for service-related issues.

Indecopi chairs the National Consumer Protection Council, an inter-institutional working group created for the integration of the local and national statutory framework on consumer protection, as well as to bolster activities carried out for the benefit of consumers and to identify common information campaigns. The Council is made up of 16 representatives from the public and private sectors: ministries, utilities regulators, business associations, and consumers associations, in co-ordination with the PCM. At the time of writing, Osinergmin has been nominated to represent all other regulators on the Council.

Legislature

The legislative branch of Peru is conferred to the Congress. The Congress is a unicameral institution composed of 130 members elected to serve five-year terms. Its current composition is the result of a reform passed in 1993 following the Democratic Constituent Congress that resulted in the new Political Constitution (OECD, 2016[1]). The Congress holds the authority to pass legislation that requires regulators to develop secondary regulations. Furthermore, the Congress can call on ministries and the regulators for them to submit opinions on draft laws and attend sessions to respond to any questions that raised by Congress. There are currently twenty-three (23) standing committees, including the Commission for Consumer Defence and Regulators of Public Utilities (*Comisión de Defensa del Consumidor y Organismos Reguladores de los Servicios Públicos*, CODECO), the Commission for Budget (*Comisión de Presupuesto y Cuenta General de la República*), and Commission for Transport and Communications (*Comisión Transporte y Comunicaciones*).

Subnational governments

There are three subnational layers of government in Peru: the regional government, the provincial local government and the district local government (OECD, 2016[2]). These government levels have exclusive and joint functions which are described in the Peruvian

Political Constitution (*Constitución Política del Perú*, CPP), the Organic Law of the Executive Power (Ley *Orgánica del Poder Ejecutivo*, LOPE, the Organic Law of Regional Governments (*Ley Orgánica de Gobiernos Regionales*, LOGR) and the Organic Law of Municipalities (*Ley Orgánica de Municipalidades*, LOM). Sub-national governments have the authority to enact regulatory measures in their region. OSIPTEL's decentralised offices (DO) are responsible for *inter alia* liaising with regional governments.

Judiciary

The judiciary is responsible for interpreting and applying the laws in Peru to ensure equal justice. It is responsible for providing mechanisms for dispute resolutions through a hierarchical system. The judiciary is led by the Supreme Court and is supported by 28 superior courts with defined jurisdictions across the 25 regions in the country. Under each superior court are 195 primary courts responsible for each province and 1 838 Courts of justice of the Peace within each district (Poder Judicial del Peru, 2012[6]). In the telecommunications sector, dispute resolution between regulated entities, as well as between regulated entities and users, are first handled via OSIPTEL's dispute resolution bodies. If the parties wish to appeal further, they can launch a "contentious administrative process" under Law No. 27584 via the judiciary. The judiciary makes the final decision on the case, which can be decided based on both the merit of the issue as well as the process. In addition, it is possible for regulated entities to utilise arbitration mechanisms for dispute resolutions, which is not part of the judiciary. Some entities prefer this route over entering into full judicial review.

Supreme audit institution

The Comptroller General of the Republic (*Contraloría General de la República del Perú,* CGR) was established in 1929 as the supreme audit institution of Peru. As the highest authority of the national control system, the CGR supervises, monitors and verifies the correct application of public policies and the use of state resources and assets. It is represented in each government body, including OSIPTEL, by the Institutional Control Body (*Órgano* de *Control Institucional,* OCI). The Chief Audit Officer of the OCI and is assigned by the General Comptroller of the Republic and its function is the correct and transparent management of resources and assets of OSIPTEL, safeguarding the legality and efficiency of its acts, as well as the achievement of its management goals, through the execution of control tasks. The rest of the audit staff are employed by the government agency. The OCI is responsible for all auditing all public spending; for example, by monitoring the procedure and evaluation process related to contracts, procurement, and other services.

Regulatory process and policy

Legislative process

Aside from the members of Congress, the President, the judiciary, autonomous public bodies, professional associations, and the citizenry are authorised to submit bills to Congress for consideration (see Figure 1.2).

Once a draft bill is submitted, it is registered by the office of the Congress and processed by the Secretary General of the executive council, who is also responsible for identifying the committee(s) that receive(s) the bill and sets the hierarchy of each committee. The assigned committee deliberates and issues a report within 30 days of reception and classifies it as favourable, unfavourable, or flat rejection. If the proposition is received by other committees, committees are welcome to submit joint or individual reports. If approved, the committee reports are received by the executive council, which includes the Secretary General, the Parliamentary Director, and the reading clerk, who will also be organising the debate and co-ordinating the distribution of the copies to the members of parliament. The plenary assembly then accepts or rejects the bill. An accepted bill is then enrolled, reviewed, and certified by the Office of the Secretary General and passed to the executive branch. The president then signs the bill into law and orders its publication, which then comes into force once published in the official gazette, *El Peruano*. If there are objections, the President may return the bill to Congress within 15 days. Without a decision from the executive within 15 days, the Congress may pass the bill into law (Congreso de la República, 2017[7]).

If within its jurisdiction, regulatory agencies are entitled to formulate secondary legislations linked to the law, following the guidelines for the regulatory quality assessment of administrative procedures (Presidencia del Consejo de Ministros, 2018[8]).

Figure 1.2. Peru's legislative process

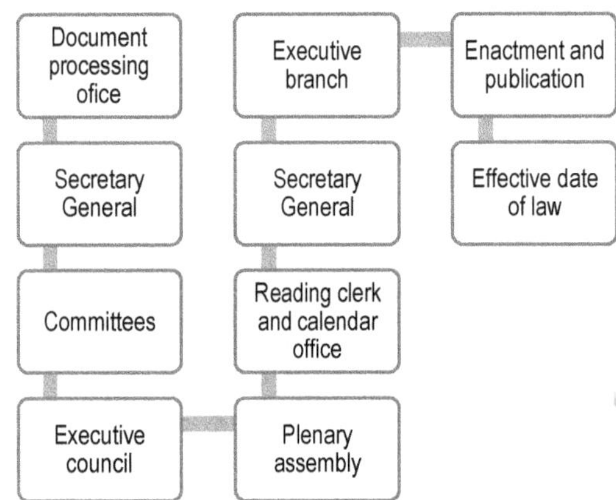

Source: (Congreso de la República, 2017[9]), *Legislative Process*, http://www.congreso.gob.pe/eng/legislative_process/ (accessed on 26 June 2018).

Rule-making process in the executive body

The executive branch has the authority to issue subordinate regulations (decrees and resolutions). It is also responsible for approving bills (draft laws) that is submitted by the President to Congress, including any legislative decrees, emergency decrees, and resolutions, as defined by law (OECD, 2016[2]).

The rule-making process in the executive is not guided by a whole-of-government policy, but certain policies and framework serve as materials in the development of regulations (see Table 1.1).

Table 1.1. Frameworks and policies that guide rule-making in the executive body

	Name	Description
Law No. 26889	Framework Law for Legislative Production and Systematisation	• Sets the general guidelines for all regulated entities when preparing bills and other proposals, e.g. purpose and rationale (*exposición de motivos*). • Regulates the nomenclature, consistency of texts (titles, articles, etc.), and the management of errata.
Law No. 27444	General Administrative Procedure Law	• Sets important rules on public consultation, including the publication of proposals
	Reglamento	• Issued by the Ministry of Justice • Regulates the publication and dissemination of regulatory proposals and regulations
	Manual of legislative technique	• Issued by the Ministry of Justice • Provides legal guidance when drafting regulations

Source: (OECD, 2016[2]), *Regulatory Policy in Peru: Assembling the Framework for Regulatory Quality*, OECD Reviews of Regulatory Reform, OECD Publishing, Paris, http://dx.doi.org/10.1787/9789264260054-en.

When issuing subordinate regulations, the common practice among ministries is to draft a proposal, guided by the frameworks and policies outlined in Table 1.1, and posted on the website for public consultation. After consultation, the head of the ministry or agency approves the regulation. For ministries, vice-ministers would also need to approve the draft before it is sent to the minister. In cases when draft regulations require approval from three or four ministries and/or agencies, the proposal must be sent to the PCM to be discussed by the vice-ministerial co-ordinating council (CCV) or adopted by the Council of Ministers before it is sent to the President of the Republic for final approval. All approved proposals are published in the official gazette, *El Peruano*. (OECD, 2016[2])

Box 1.2. OECD Regulatory Policy Review of Peru

In 2016, the OECD conducted a review of the regulatory policy of Peru to assess the policies, institutions, and tools utilised by the government and regulatory bodies in the country in designing, implementing, and enforcing high-quality regulations. This review formed part of the OECD Peru country programme along with four other reviews of sectoral public policy in Peru.

The report provides an overall assessment of the political context of regulatory reform carried out by oversight bodies and relevant regulatory agencies in the country. It recognises the progress achieved to date, including the numerous tools and activities – such as a broad administrative simplification programme – utilised to improve the regulatory environment in the country. The report also highlights the challenges and improvements that remain in order to achieve a world-class regulatory framework and provides a set of recommendations and next steps, including:

- establishing a **regulatory oversight body**, as a way to create more coherence in regulatory policy activities and tools across ministries, agencies, and offices;
- issuing a **policy statement** – either through a law or a binding legal document – on regulatory policy, with clear objectives, strategies, and tools when managing the entire regulatory governance cycle;
- measuring **administrative burdens** created by formalities and information obligations;

- making **inspection and enforcement of regulations** an integral part of the regulatory policy framework, including through developing a set of guidelines related to ethical behaviour and corruption prevention;
- promoting a **coherent national regulatory framework** that actively encourages the adoption and use of regulatory tools and best-practice sharing.

In addition, the report provides a brief overview of the governance arrangements of regulators and their interactions with the central government. It underscores the degree of independence exerted by regulators on budget and decision making, their transparency and accountability mechanisms, as well as an overview of the regulatory policy tools applied throughout the policy cycle. Economic regulators are considered to implement more sophisticated tools than other government bodies and have progressively improved its adoption and implementation.

Following the report, the Presidency of the Council of Ministers (PCM) has been proactive in developing initiatives and co-ordinating with ministries and regulatory bodies to improve the national regulatory framework. For example, in 2017, the PCM developed a set of guidelines for the regulatory quality assessment of administrative procedures to further improve the regulatory environment for citizens and businesses. The guidelines aim to guide government bodies under their purview in identifying, reducing and measuring administrative burdens created by formalities and information obligations in both the local and the national level.

Source: (OECD, 2016[2]), *Regulatory Policy in Peru: Assembling the Framework for Regulatory Quality*, OECD Reviews of Regulatory Reform, OECD Publishing, Paris, http://dx.doi.org/10.1787/9789264260054-en.

Sector context and main regulatory reforms

The telecommunications law enacted in 1991 created OSIPTEL as the economic regulator to lead the transformation and modernisation of the telecommunications sector and, in 1994, replaced the Committee of the Regulation of Telecommunications Tariffs. The privatisation of two state telephone companies, *Compañía Peruana de Teléfonos* (CPT) and *Empresa Nacional de Telecomunicaciones* (ENTEL), in 1994 also paved the way towards the modernisation of the Peruvian telecommunications sector.[8]

Prior to OSIPTEL's creation, limited and inefficient coverage of telecommunications services was an issue, notably in the rural areas. During its first years of operation, OSIPTEL's objectives were to increase investment, geographic coverage and quality of services. It also set the first consumer protection frameworks for the sector, including information relating to the design of user service platforms as well as maximum timelines for service solutions. The regulator's and the government's overarching goal of improving services in rural areas was supported with the creation of the Telecommunications Fund (*Fondo de inversion en telecomunicaciones*, FITEL) (Box 1.3)

Box 1.3. Telecommunications Investment Fund (FITEL)

The Telecommunications Investment Fund (*Fondo de Inversión en Telecomunicaciones*, FITEL) was established through Peruvian Telecommunications Law Supreme Decree 013-93 in 1994 and originally administered by OSIPTEL. In 2006, the Fund was transferred from OSIPTEL to the Ministry of Transport and Communications (MTC). FITEL is aimed at facilitating universal access to essential telecommunications services in rural areas and places of social interest.[1]

FITEL is managed by a three-member decision-making body: the President is the Minister of Transport and Communications, while the Minister of Economy and Finance and the President of OSIPTEL serve as the other members. FITEL is staffed with 120 people who carry out policy formulation, promotion and supervision functions. Policy is set by the MTC, while formulation is guided by MEF principles that require social and economic viability as well as benefit for the country. Promotion is also carried out in accordance with rules set by MEF.

The Fund subsidises the installation, operation, and use of public telecommunications services in the rural areas to achieve universal access. It is sourced from 1% of the gross income of service operators and carriers in the telecommunications sector as well as fines collected from non-compliance or violations. In 2018, the total budget for FITEL was nearly PEN 400 million.

Projects financed by FITEL include telecommunications projects and studies presented through a public tender by ProInversión. These projects can focus on activities related to investments in infrastructure, operation, maintenance and supervision, skills development, as well as procurement and purchase of new equipment or technology. The individual or enterprise with the lowest required subsidy wins the bidding process. (OSIPTEL, 2014[10])

Projects are prioritised in accordance with an annual plan. OSIPTEL attends monthly meetings with FITEL decision-making body, which allows them to present proposals for projects for approval and funding. To date, FITEL has carried out over 27 projects in the country and are currently executing 11 projects as of August 2018 (investment phase), with the majority focused on improving broadband connectivity in identified areas (FITEL, 2018[11]) to provide internet for health, education and security purposes.

Projects are deployed using either Public-Private Partnerships (PPPs) or Projects in Assets (*Proyectos en Activos*), which allows ministries, regional governments and local governments to promote private investments of assets owned by the respective Private Investment Promotion Board (*Organismo Promotor de la Inversión Privada*, OPIP). For projects implemented under the latter scheme, OSIPTEL cannot issue binding opinions over issues that intersect with their competencies, i.e. concession contracts, tariffs, quality of service, essential facilities, and competition. OSIPTEL can also be tasked with creating ad hoc regulations in accordance with specific projects. Moreover, for telecommunications projects implemented under this scheme, responsibility for supervising the quality of services is assigned to FITEL, which can run the risk of duplicating efforts with OSIPTEL who supervise quality of service in all other areas of the telecommunications sector.

1. Qualified rural areas are based on the definition provided by the National Statistics and Information Institute (*Instituto Nacional de Estadísticañ e Informática*, INEI): (1) are less than 3 000 inhabitants (as measured by INEI); (2) have a shortage of basic services; and (3) have less than 2% of telephone density. Places of social interest include: (1) population centres first to third quintile of the poverty map, as defined by the Social Development and Compensation Fund (*Fondo de Cooperación para el Desarrollo Social*, FONCODES); (2) do not have at least 1 public service for essential telecommunications services; (3) have less than 1 public telephone line per 500 inhabitants; or (4) are localities located in the border districts. (MTC, 2010[12]).

Source: (MTC, 2010[13]), *FITEL Telecomunicaciones para áreas rurales de Perú Agenda • ¿Qué es FITEL?*, http://www.cedecap.org.pe/uploads/archivos/mesaplanesnacionales_irmamora-fitel.pdf (accessed on 05 November 2018); (OSIPTEL, 2014[10]), *The Telecommunications Boom*, OSIPTEL, https://www.osiptel.gob.pe/Archivos/Publicaciones/boom_telecomunicaciones/boom_telecomunicaciones_osiptel.html#6, (FITEL, 2018[11]), *Estado de los Proyectos del Fitel*, http://www.fitel.gob.pe/pg/proyectos-supervision.php (accessed on 22 June 2018); (MEF, n.d.[14]), *Proyectos en Activos*, https://www.mef.gob.pe/index.php?option=com_content&view=article&id=4437&Itemid=102247&lang=es (accessed on 02 November 2018), (MTC, 2010[12]), *FITEL: Telecomunicaciones para áreas rurales de Perú*, http://www.cedecap.org.pe/uploads/archivos/mesaplanesnacionales_irmamora-fitel.pdf (accessed on 22 June 2018).

In the 1990s, users had to pay for both calls initiated and received, which greatly constrained the expansion of public telecommunications services. Based on analysis and consultations, OSIPTEL introduced a new rate system that passed the cost to the calling party for fixed and mobile services in 1996 (OSIPTEL, 2014, p. 68[10]). This reform resulted in an increase of mobile-to-mobile and fixed-to-mobile traffic as well as a reduction of rates in the medium-term. Following the arrival of new operators in the fixed market, OSIPTEL established price cap rate formula that reduced rates on a quarterly basis and, through a productivity factor, transferred efficiency improvements obtained by the company to the users. A number of reforms followed suit, including those regulating long distance calls, public payphones, and fee collection.

For the first decade of existence, OSIPTEL's mandate was focused on transitioning to a liberalised telecommunications market through promoting competition and facilitating new entrants into the market. Up to the early- to md-2000s, several companies entered the mobile market, namely TIM, Nextel, Bellsouth and America Móvil. TIM was later acquired by America Móvil, and Bellsouth was acquired by Telefonica. As of 2018, America Movil and Telefonica are still in the market, while in 2014 Nextel became ENTEL and Viettel entered the market.

Expansion of operators was part of a larger effort to expand services, especially in the mobile sector, that lasted from 2005 to 2014. Over this period, the quantity of districts with coverage went from less than 500 to more than 1 500. Following this period, OSIPTEL's mandate shifted towards a regulatory policy concentrated on strengthening competition through access conditions and setting prices of essential facilities to promote rapid and efficient entry to the market. Most recently, this mandate has focused on promoting competition in the mobile markets and reducing barriers to entry, namely in regards to reducing costs for consumers to switch providers. This mandate is reflected in the regulator's current slogan: *promovemos la competencia y empoderamos al usuario* (we promote competition and empower the user).

Even after OSIPTEL efforts, there were lots of uncover areas. Thus, other major reforms of the regulatory framework delivered by OSIPTEL include those in relation to the 2012 broadband policy via the establishment of the national fibre optical backbone (*Red Dorsal Nacional de Fibra Optica,* RDNFO) and promotion of broadband connections. Figure 1.3 describes other major reforms implemented by OSIPTEL to improve sector performance.

Figure 1.3. Major reforms to promote competition in the telecommunications sector

1996	• Regulation concerning leasing of circuits
1998	• Approval of the Interconnection regulations
1999	• Long distance: Implementation of the "pre-selection" and "call by call" system
2000	• Regulation on terminating calls in fixed lines networks based on an efficient company model
2001	• Application of the price caps rate formula as of 2001 and review of the productivity factor every three years • Regulation of public payphones access charge
2003	• Review of terminating fee in fixed lines networks, based on costs model
2004	• Regulation on billing and collection fees between operators
2007	• Regulation on developing and expanding mobile network infrastructures (updated in 2015)
2010	• Mobile number portability
2012	• Broadband policy • General conditions for the provision of complementary facilities to carrier services of the RDNFO • Regulation on access fees to the complementary access facility
2014	• Update of the quality of service regulatory framework • Mobile & fixed number portability (first available in 2010 for mobile, but relaunched in 2014 to include fixed) • Prohibition on the sale of blocked mobile phones
2015	• Price caps for the regional transport service and for internet access of public institutions

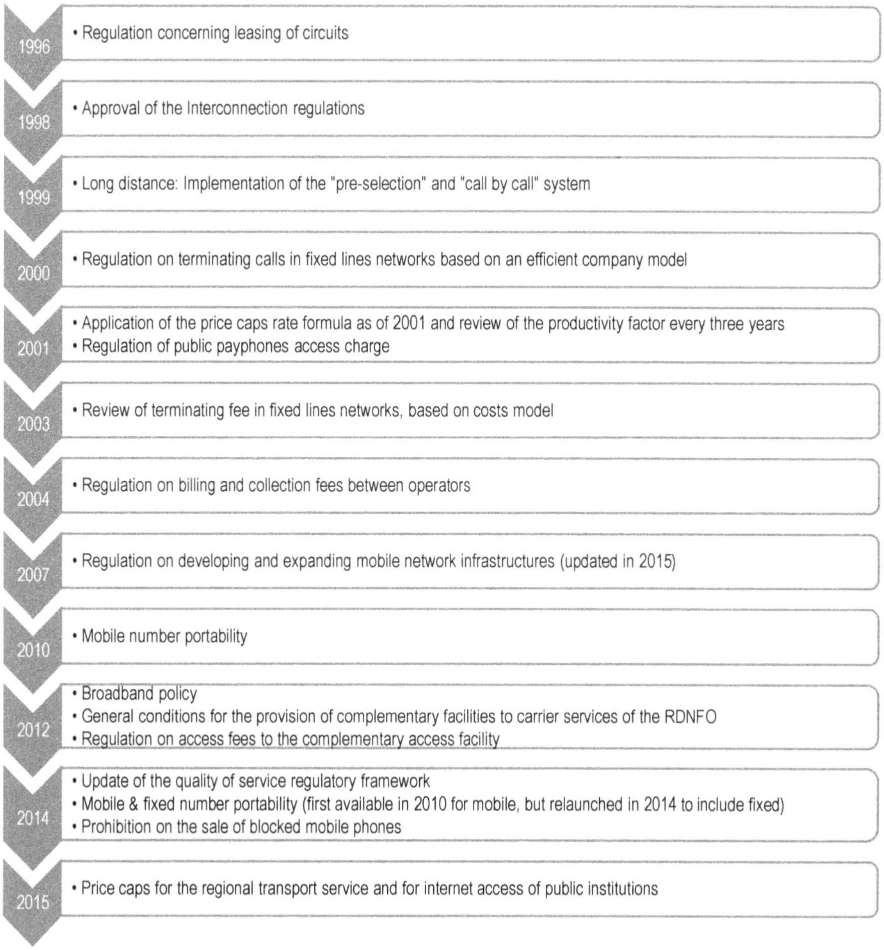

Source: (OSIPTEL, 2014[15]), *El Boom de las Telecomunicaciones - OSIPTEL*, https://www.osiptel.gob.pe/Archivos/Publicaciones/boom_telecomunicaciones/files/assets/basic-html/index.html#1/z#noFlash (accessed on 22 June 2018).

The Peruvian telecommunications sector underwent one of the most dynamic modernisation processes in the country, linked to the advent and growth of new services (mobile telephony and internet) and the arrival of new providers to the market. As of 2018, there are 5 large operators and more than 100 small- and medium-sized enterprises providing telecommunication services in the country, with Telefónica as the largest player and leader in mobile telephony. Table 1.2 shows the number of users for all sub-sectors in 2018, Figure 1.4 demonstrates the growth of fixed and mobile lines from 1994 to 2018, and Figure 1.5 shows the evolution of market concentration for mobile telephony 2014-17. UN statistics show that Peru's population in 2017 was over 32 million, while the number of households was 8.3 million (Euromonitor International, 2018[16]).

Table 1.2. Users by telecommunication subsector (March 2018)

Sub-sector	Number of users
Mobile lines	40 020 419
Mobile internet	22 920 990
Fixed telephone	2 930 161
Fixed internet	2 350 218
Pay television	1 979 762

Note: Consistent data on mobile internet was not available at the time of writing this report. According to (Euromonitor International, 2018[16]), total population of Peru in 2017 was approximately 32 million people.
Source: Information provided by OSIPTEL, 2018.

Figure 1.4. Growth of fixed and mobile lines in service in Peru, 1994-2013

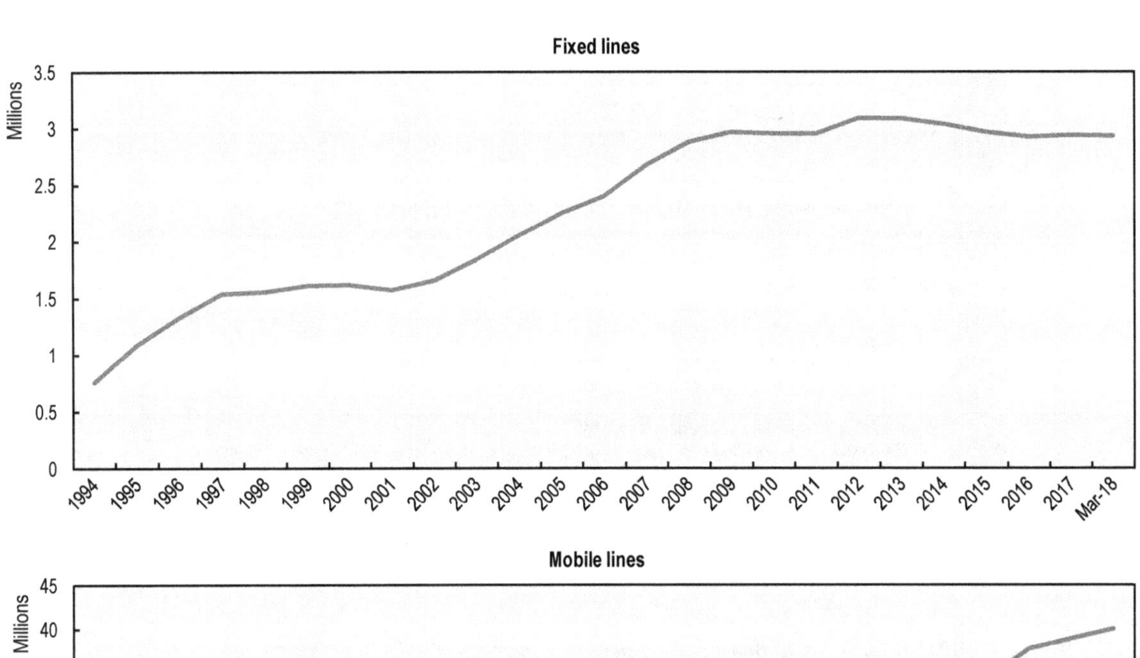

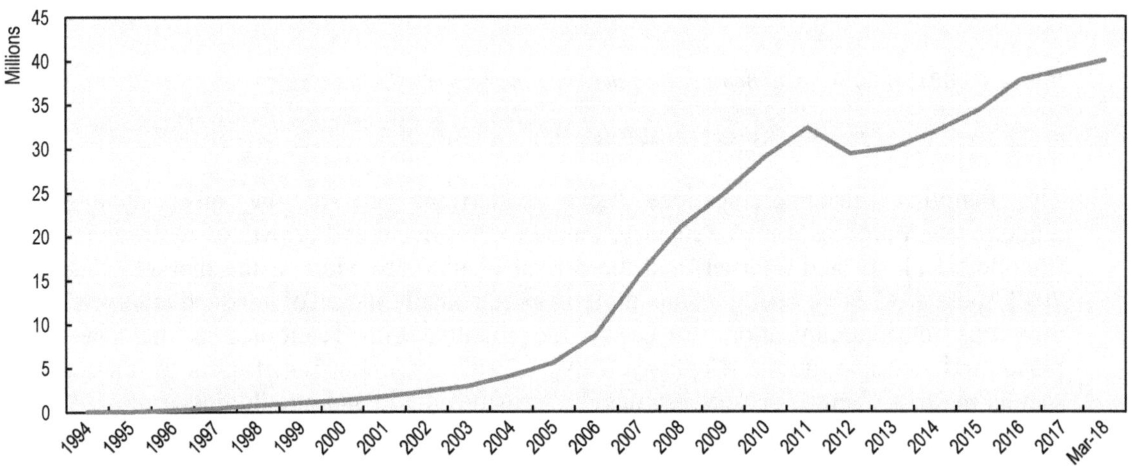

Source: (OSIPTEL, 2014[15]), *El Boom de las Telecomunicaciones - OSIPTEL*, https://www.osiptel.gob.pe/Archivos/Publicaciones/boom_telecomunicaciones/files/assets/basic-html/index.html#1/z#noFlash (accessed on 22 June 2018).

Figure 1.5. Evolution of market concentration in mobile telephony, 2014-17

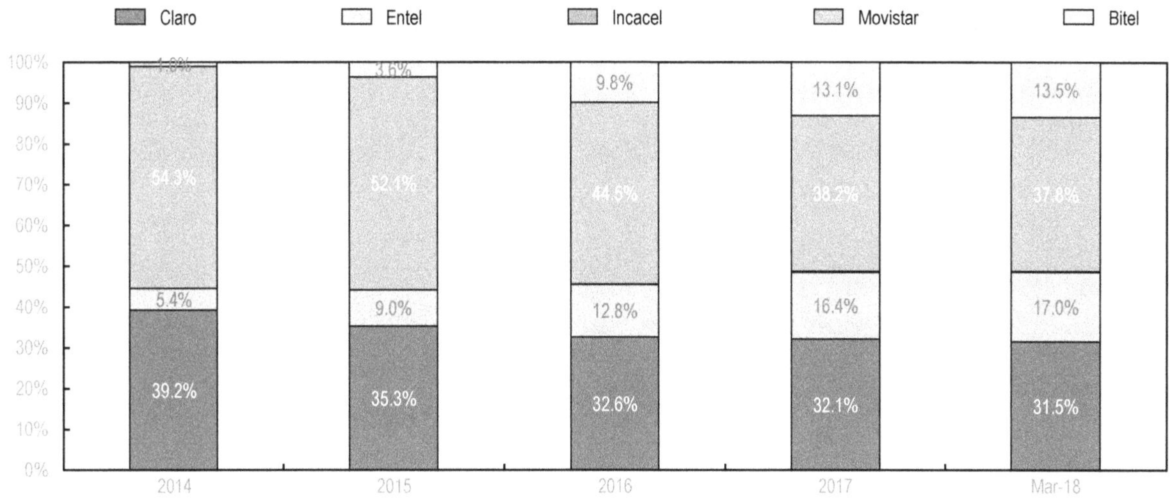

Source: (OSIPTEL, 2018[17]), *Reporte Estadístico - Febrero 2018*, https://www.osiptel.gob.pe/Archivos/Publicaciones/reporte-estadistico_feb2018/files/assets/basic-html/index.html#1 (accessed on 22 June 2018).

Mobile penetration is notably high in urban areas. In contrast, there remains an urban-rural divide in terms of access to fixed or fixed-to-mobile services, owing to the challenging geographical landscape as well as size of the country and remote location of smaller, more insulated communities. The rural population has diminished in relative terms, representing 22.5% of the total Peruvian population in 2017, compared to 28% in 2007.

Notes

[1] Some public sector agencies are exempted from SERVIR's policies, as defined by Legislative Decree 1023.

[2] See more: https://www.mef.gob.pe/es/evaluaciones-de-impacto.

[3] The regulator was operating under the name OSINERG until 2007, when it was extended to cover the mining subsector and was then renamed OSINERGMIN.

[4] SUNASS was created by the Law Decree No. 25965 of December 19th, 1992; OSIPTEL by the Legislative Decree No. 702 of July 11th, 1991; OSINERGMIN by the Law No. 26734 of December 31st, 1996; and OSITRAN by Law No. 26917 of 23 January 1998.

[5] Indecopi was created by Executive Order No. 25868 of November 1992. Act 27444 and Legislative Decree No. 1256 serve as the legal basis for their methodology and approach.

[6] The only exception across all regulated sectors is telecommunications, where competition law powers rest with the economic regulator (OSIPTEL) instead.

[7] Article No. 110 of Law 29571, Code for the Protection and Defense of the Consumer. A cap for micro- and small-enterprises is set at 10% and 20%, respectively, of sales or gross income received.

[8] Prior to 1994, CPT provided telephony services to metropolitan Lima and ENTEL offered national d and international services (OSIPTEL, 2014[16]).

References

CEPLAN (2018), *Politicas y Planes*, http://www.ceplan.gob.pe/politicas-y-planes/ (accessed on 22 June 2018). [3]

CEPLAN (2018), *Qué es el Sinaplan?*, http://www.ceplan.gob.pe/sinaplan/ (accessed on 22 June 2018). [4]

Congreso de la República (2017), *How does a bill become a law?*, http://www.congreso.gob.pe/eng/legislative_process/ (accessed on 26 June 2018). [7]

Congreso de la República (2017), *Legislative Process*, http://www.congreso.gob.pe/eng/legislative_process/ (accessed on 26 June 2018). [9]

Euromonitor International (2018), *Peru Country Factfile*, https://www.euromonitor.com/peru/country-factfile (accessed on 29 August 2018). [16]

FITEL (2018), *Estado de los Proyectos del Fitel*, http://www.fitel.gob.pe/pg/proyectos-supervision.php (accessed on 22 June 2018). [11]

MEF (n.d.), *Proyectos en Activos*, https://www.mef.gob.pe/index.php?option=com_content&view=article&id=4437&Itemid=102247&lang=es (accessed on 02 November 2018). [14]

MTC (2010), *FITEL Telecomunicaciones para áreas rurales de Perú Agenda • ¿Qué es FITEL?*, http://www.cedecap.org.pe/uploads/archivos/mesaplanesnacionales_irmamora-fitel.pdf (accessed on 05 November 2018). [13]

MTC (2010), *FITEL: Telecomunicaciones para áreas rurales de Perú*, http://www.cedecap.org.pe/uploads/archivos/mesaplanesnacionales_irmamora-fitel.pdf (accessed on 22 June 2018). [12]

OECD (2016), *Multi-dimensional Review of Peru: Volume 2. In-depth Analysis and Recommendations*, OECD Development Pathways, OECD Publishing, Paris, http://dx.doi.org/10.1787/9789264264670-en. [5]

OECD (2016), *OECD Public Governance Reviews: Peru: Integrated Governance for Inclusive Growth*, OECD Public Governance Reviews, OECD Publishing, Paris, http://dx.doi.org/10.1787/9789264265172-en. [1]

OECD (2016), *Regulatory Policy in Peru: Assembling the Framework for Regulatory Quality*, OECD Reviews of Regulatory Reform, OECD Publishing, Paris, http://dx.doi.org/10.1787/9789264260054-en. [2]

OSIPTEL (2018), *Reporte Estadístico - Febrero 2018*, https://www.osiptel.gob.pe/Archivos/Publicaciones/reporte-estadistico_feb2018/files/assets/basic-html/index.html#1 (accessed on 22 June 2018). [17]

OSIPTEL (2014), *El Boom de las Telecomunicaciones - OSIPTEL*, https://www.osiptel.gob.pe/Archivos/Publicaciones/boom_telecomunicaciones/files/assets/basic-html/index.html#1/z#noFlash (accessed on 22 June 2018). [15]

OSIPTEL (2014), *The Telecommunications Boom*, OSIPTEL, https://www.osiptel.gob.pe/Archivos/Publicaciones/boom_telecomunicaciones/boom_telecomunicaciones_osiptel.html#6. [10]

Poder Judicial del Peru (2012), *Poder Judicial del Peru*, http://www.pj.gob.pe/wps/wcm/connect/CorteSuprema/s_cortes_suprema_home/as_Inicio/ (accessed on 25 June 2018). [6]

Presidencia del Consejo de Ministros (2018), *Guidelines for the Regulatory Quality Assessment of Administrative Procedures*. [8]

Chapter 2. Governance of Peru's telecommunications regulator

The Performance Assessment Framework for Economic Regulators (PAFER) was developed by the OECD to help regulators assess their own performance. The PAFER structures the drivers of performance along an input-process-output-outcome framework. This chapter applies the framework to the governance of Peru's telecommunications regulator (Organismo Supervisor de Inversión Privada en Telecomunicaciones, OSIPTEL) and reviews the existing features, opportunities and challenges faced by OSIPTEL in developing an effective performance assessment framework.

Role and objectives

The Supervisory Agency for Private Investment in Telecommunications (*Organismo Supervisor de Inversión Privada en Telecomunicaciones,* OSIPTEL) was created on 11 July 1991 by the Legislative Decree No. 702 with the goal of protecting the telecommunication public services market from practices against free and fair competition. Its creation was part of a wave of structural reforms in the early 1990s as Peru moved towards a liberalised economic model. This liberalisation was accompanied by the creation of government bodies to manage the new economy, including independent regulators for four key sectors – telecommunications, energy, water and sanitation, and transportation.

OSIPTEL officially began its operations in 1994, with the installation of its first set of Board of Directors. Since then, the mandate of the agency has been to regulate and supervise the telecommunications market in Peru. OSIPTEL has the authority to fix the tariff structure, manage and issue regulatory instruments, mediate and settle complaints at the second instance and settle controversies between operators at the first and second instance, and establish and impose sanctions and corrective measures. The regulator is also the competition authority for the telecommunications sector, a function exercised by Indecopi, Peru's competition and consumer protection authority, for most other sectors of the country's economy. Reportedly, this distinction is due to a need for higher specialised knowledge of the sector in the case of telecommunications. A summary of the regulatory framework governing OSIPTEL's roles and objectives can be found in Box 2.1.

Box 2.1. OSIPTEL's regulatory framework

OSIPTEL is governed by general rules that apply to all for Peruvian regulators, as well as specific rules that govern only OSIPTEL.

Common regulations governing Peruvian regulators

- Law No. 27332, Framework Law on Regulatory Agencies for Private Investment in Public Utilities (*Ley Marco de los Organismos Reguladores de la Inversión Privada en los Servicios Públicos,* LMOR).
- Supreme Decree No. 042-2005-PCM (LMOR regulations).

The LMOR and its regulations establish characteristics, functions and main organisational rules for Peruvian regulators. For example, the LMOR defines regulators as entities with administrative, functional, technical, economic and financial autonomy. In addition, the LMOR grants them with their functions, as noted in Table 2.1. It also establishes the rules that govern the Board of Directors rules and the Users Councils (*Consejo de Usuarios*).

Rules specific to OSIPTEL

- Legislative Decree No. 702: Creates OSIPTEL as Peru's telecommunications regulator. OSIPTEL oversees the efficiency and quality of the telecommunications services and protects the users and markets from unfair competition practices.
- Supreme Decree No. 013-93-TCC, Telecommunications Law: Regulates OSIPTEL's general and specific functions, such as approving standards for interconnection agreements.
- Law No. 27336 (*Ley de Desarrollo de las Funciones y Facultades de OSIPTEL*):

Law that establishes precisions to OSIPTEL's functions, including regulations to strengthen enforcement and inspections.

- Supreme Decree No. 008-2001-PCM (*Reglamento General de OSIPTEL*): Law that develops in more depth LMOR and Law No. 27336 regulations, regarding functions and the regulator's internal organisation.
- Resolution of the Board of Directors No. 032-2002 (*Reglamento de Organización y Funciones*): Internal organisation and functions regulations.

Source: OECD analysis based on information provided by OSIPTEL, 2018.

OSIPTEL's main legal powers are indicated in the Law No. 27332, Framework Law on Regulatory Agencies for Private Investment in Public Utilities (*Ley Marco de los Organismos Reguladores de la Inversión Privada en los Servicios Públicos,* LMOR), enacted in 2000. This law allows regulators, such as OSIPTEL, to supervise, regulate, establish norms, and inspect the sector activity of regulated entities and serve as the competition authority in the sector (see Table 2.1). In contrast, the Ministry of Transport and Communications (*Ministerio de Transportes y Comunicaciones*, MTC) set sector policy and perform some regulatory and supervision functions (see Table 2.2).

Table 2.1. Powers and functions of OSIPTEL

Competition	Promotes competition between telecommunications operators by reducing barriers to entry and reducing costs for consumers to switch providers
Tariff-setting	Sets tariffs and quality standards/obligations for public utilities in the telecommunications sector
Regulatory	Establishes norms and rules, define infractions and set sanctions
Enforcement and inspections	Qualifies infractions and impose sanctions
Conflict resolution	Resolves disputes in telecommunications sector
Claim resolution	Acts as second instance for customer claims
Supervisory	Supervises that regulated entities respect sector norms and regulations emitted by the regulator

Source: (OSIPTEL, 2018[1]), *Plan Estratégico Institucional 2018-22*, OSIPTEL, https://www.osiptel.gob.pe/repositorioaps/data/1/1/1/PAR/res025-2018-pd/Res025-2018-PD_PEI2018-2022.pdf (accessed on 22 June 2018).

Table 2.2. Powers and functions of the MTC

Policy	Defines sector policy
Regulatory	Defines technical/industry and service standards, issues/revokes licenses of operators,
Entry	Assigns numbering and in charge of spectrum policy
Enforcement and inspections	Imposes structural remedies, investigates breaches of law and imposes sanctions (in co-operator with the regulator)
Supervisory	Enforces compliance with standards and regulations, vetoes investment plans of operators

Source: Information provided by OSIPTEL, 2018.

OSIPTEL as an institution has progressively evolved according to changes in the market – from public companies to limited competition in basic services, to competition in all services and, from 2006 to present, the consolidation of markets (see Figure 2.1). This was influenced by a period of rapid technological advances and the development of new sectors in the telecommunications sector.

Figure 2.1. Evolution of OSIPTEL's role in the telecommunications market in Peru

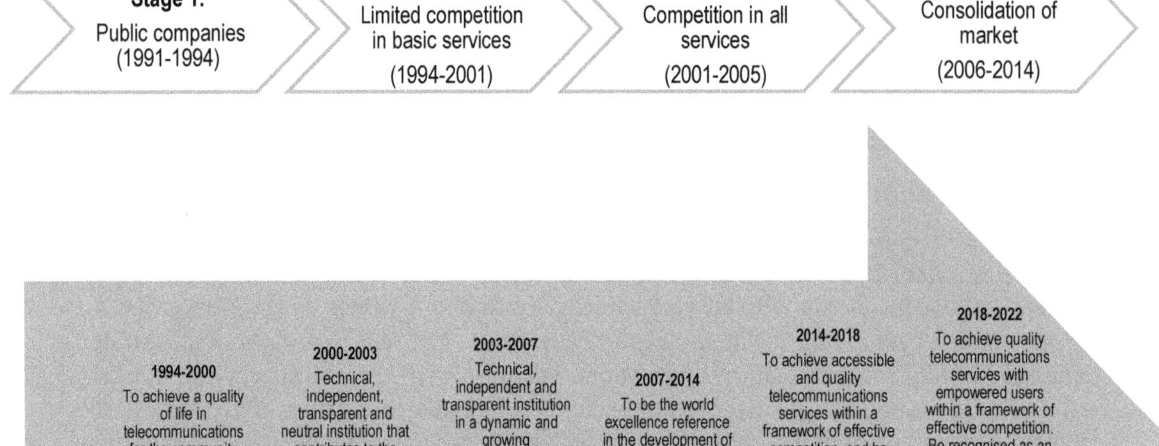

Source: Information provided by OSIPTEL, 2018.

Institutional co-ordination

The functions of OSIPTEL, the MTC, Congress and other regulatory and public administration bodies (Table 2.3) are contained in their respective organic laws published in the Official Gazette, *El Peruano,* and publicly available on the respective websites of each entity and the national portal of the Peruvian state. These entities can initiate activities that impact the regulator's duties and functions, ranging from national security policy by the Ministry of Interior or the national data policy by the Ministry of Justice, to legislations passed by Congress that will require the regulator to pass corresponding secondary legislation.

The relationship between these entities is governed by the principle of effective collaboration through agreements of inter-institutional collaboration that facilitate activities of co-ordination and mutual co-operation.[1] There are no structured co-ordination mechanisms with other public administration bodies, including the other economic regulators. Co-ordination is often facilitated rather through ad hoc channels based on personal relationships established between senior officials at OSIPTEL and the public administration bodies.

Table 2.3. Public administration bodies involved in the telecommunications sector in Peru

Institution	Role	Interactions with OSIPTEL
Congress	Unicameral legislative branch of 130 members.	Has the power to request OSIPTEL to provide comments on issues or draft laws in either full plenary or in two standing committees – the Transport and Communications Committee and the Defense of Consumers and Regulatory Bodies Commission (CODECO)
Presidency of the Council of Ministers (PCM)	Responsible for co-ordinating national and sectoral policies within the executive branch	Oversees and provides guidance on the general administrative processes, key role in nominating and appointing Board members, administering budget allocations and disbursements.
Ministry of Economy and Finance (MEF)	Developing economic and financial policy for Peru, including co-ordinating the performance-budgeting system	OSIPTEL must report on indicators regard their yearly operational plan (*Plan Operativo Institucional,* POI) through the performance-budgeting system
Ministry of Transport and Communications (MTC)	Defining and developing policies for Peru's transportation systems and telecommunications sector	The MTC established general sector policy, as well as performs some regulatory and supervisory functions, and oversees various projects, such as the Telecommunications Investment Fund (FITEL). Can request OSIPTEL to provide comments on issues or draft laws and regulations.
Telecommunications Investment Fund (FITEL)	Subsidises the installation, operation and use of public telecommunications services in rural areas and is funded by levies on service operators and carriers as well as fines collected from supervisions	OSIPTEL participates in non-binding discussions related to investments and supervises contracts
Proinversion	Specialised technical body attached to the MEF responsible for the promotion of national investments through public-private partnerships (PPPs) in services, infrastructure, assets, and other state projects	Can receive non-binding comments from OSIPTEL when developing investment projects
Indecopi	Independent regulatory body aimed at both providing competition and consumer protection.	Has the authority to issue binding decisions and levy penalties on regulators or decisions taken by OSIPTEL, as well as conduct *ex post* reviews of regulations enacted by OSIPTEL and under the jurisdiction of Indecopi.
Ministry of Interior	Oversees issues related to national security, including civil defence	New national security laws have recently given the Ministry requirements and authority to promote national and cross-border network and telecommunications security
Ministry of Justice	Oversees judicial matters in Peru	Oversees the role of the courts, including the process of appeals and judicial review through which OSIPTEL's actions can be challenged. Proposes an attorney general for all public institutions.

Source: Prepared by the OECD Based on information collected during the review, 2018.

OSIPTEL can receive requests for information or opinions from any of these bodies and lack of co-ordination make it challenging to respond in an appropriate amount of time, especially when more than one request is made in the same time period.

To foster effective collaboration, OSIPTEL has been active in developing national, regional and international co-operation agreements with various government bodies and telecommunications regulatory agencies (see Table 2.4).

Table 2.4. Agreements signed by OSIPTEL with other telecommunications regulatory agencies

Within Peru	LAC region	Outside LAC region	International bodies
• Central Reserve Bank of Peru • Various regional and local governments • Other regulators (Osinergmin, OSITRAN, SUNASS, and Indecopi) • National Registry of Identification and Marital Status (RENIEC)	• Bolivia: Transports and Telecommunications Regulation and Enforcement Agency (ATT) • Brazil: National Telecommunications Agency (ANATEL) • Dominican Republic: Dominican Telecommunications Institute (INDOTEL) • Ecuador: National Secretariat of Telecommunications (SENATEL) • Ecuador: Ministry of Telecommunications and Information Society (MINTEL) • Mexico: Federal Telecommunications Institute (IFT)	• France: Association Echanges et Consultations Techniques Internationaux (ECTI) • United States: Federal Communications Commission (FCC) • United States: Qualcomm	• International Telecommunications Union (ITU)

Source: Information provided by OSIPTEL, 2018.

Functions

OSIPTEL performs functions related to promoting competition, advising other government agencies, and protecting consumers in the telecommunications sector. The functions of OSIPTEL have increased over time, linked in part to changes in the sector. The MTC, Congress and other executive agencies can also add functions to OSIPTEL through legislative text without granting additional resources to implement these new functions. OSIPTEL estimates that 14 such functions have been granted to them since 2013 (see Table 2.5). OSIPTEL expended PEN 5.5 million of their budget in 2017 on these new functions. Two functions – the Rural Mobile Infrastructure Operators (OIMR) and procedures for the removal of telecommunications infrastructure – were most recently assumed and OSIPTEL does not yet have an estimation for how much it will cost to implement.

Table 2.5. New functions added to OSIPTEL since 2013

• Supervise the obligations contained in the concession contract between Telefónica del Peru with the Peruvian State
• Increased monitoring of procurement issues (biometric/non-biometric system) and citizen security.
• Regulation and supervision of the National Fiber Optic Dorsal Network (RDNFO).
• Regulation and supervision of Regional Projects (transport and access networks).
• Systematization and digitization of user complaints.
• Greater load of activities due to the operation of the RENTESEG.
• Supervising the blocking of mobile telephone signals in prisons
• Access of electronic money issuers to mobile services
• Access by Mobile Virtual Operators (MVNOs) to the networks of telecommunications concessionaires.
• Rural Mobile Infrastructure Operators (OIMR)
• Supervising the Quality Regulation and Coverage Regulation (integrates Internet supervision and supervision in rural areas)
• Obligations of concessionaires to geolocate mobile equipment
• Developing and monitoring compliance with network neutrality legislation
• Create a mandatory procedure for the removal of telecommunications infrastructure that may interfere with the execution of infrastructure works

Source: Information provided by OSIPTEL, 2018.

Competition functions

Competition functions are carried out by the Regulatory Policy and Competition Department *(Gerencia de Políticas Regulatorias y Competencia*, GPRC), who focus on *ex ante* competition promotion and also maintain data and conduct analyses of market competition and development. This includes developing general regulations for the telecommunications market, including setting prices, tariffs, and interconnection charges. OSIPTEL also considers deregulation if they consider that the particular problem had already been solved.

Ex post competition functions are also carried out by OSIPTEL through the application of the competition laws in the telecommunications market, namely the Law on the Repression of Anti-competitive Behaviours (*Ley de Represión de Conductas Anticompetitivas*) and the Law of Repression of Unfair Competition (*Ley de Represión de la Competencia Desleal*). These laws are applied through sanctions and corrective measures. The Technical Secretariat also carries out *ex officio* investigations to detect anticompetitive or unfair behavior between operators, which are heard by the Collegiate Bodies in the first instance and Controversies Settlement Court in the second instance (see more in the Appeals section).

Prices are regulated in the fixed line and wholesale markets to create accurate conditions for the development of public utilities in the telecommunications sector and ensure quality and economic efficiency. OSIPTEL is reviewing the need to continue regulating fixed lines. The General Tariff Regulation (*Reglamento General de Tarifas*, RGT) and the Procedure for Setting and Reviewing Price Caps (*Procedimiento de Fijación y Revision de Tarifas Tope*) establish the methodologies for price-setting.

When regulated, prices are set every four years but can be reviewed every two years upon the request of a regulated entity or due to significant changes in the market. These are set through cost models based on cost-oriented price caps, international benchmarking, simulations of hypothetically efficient firms, cost-models from regulated entities, or a specific model of particular need.

Regulatory interventions can be initiates in response to: 1) laws enacted by Congress; 2) requests by the MTC, executive entities, or stakeholders; or 3) a detected market failure. For the first and second sources, OSIPTEL can be requested to accept new responsibilities without additional budget or staffing.

While OSIPTEL is the competition agency for telecommunications, some of these functions are assigned to the MTC. This includes licensing new operators in the market and determining when and how spectrum is auctioned. MTC usually consults with OSIPTEL with regards to spectrum auctions to receive a non-binding opinion on anti-competitiveness concerns. No merger law exists currently in Peru; the only merger control is with those involving a transfer of spectrum, which are decided upon by the MTC with non-binding opinion from OSIPTEL.

Advisory functions

The MTC can solicit technical support from the OSIPTEL, which the regulator does regularly and informally. Channels include commenting on open consultations, or receiving an ad hoc request from the Ministry for the regulator's high level of technical expertise and capacity on a certain issue. The MTC can also comment on OSIPTEL's open consultations. However, OSIPTEL's technical opinions on Ministry consultations are non-binding in nature and in several instances the Ministry has acted contrary to the regulator's recommendations (see Table 2.6). Non-binding opinions can also be requested by Congress and other ministries on measures to restore or promote competition.

Table 2.6. Decisions by MTC on mergers and spectrum allocation (2004-2018)

Year	Operators involved		OSIPTEL's opinion	Final MTC decision
2004	Telefónica del Peru	BellSouth	In favour, with conditions	Approved
2011	America Móvil	Telmex	In favour, with conditions	Approved
2011 2013 (new request)	Telefónica del Peru	Telefónica Móviles, T. Multimedia, Star Global Com	In favour, with conditions	Approved
2014	Americatel	Nextel	In favour	Approved
2014 (pure spectrum transfer)	Telefónica del Peru	America Móvil	Disagree	Approved
2015 (merger with spectrum transfer)	TC Siglo 21	TVS Wireless	Disagree	Approved
2016 (merger with spectrum transfer)	OLO	TVS Wireless	Disagree	Approved
2017 (merge with spectrum transfer)	TC Siglo 21	OLO	Disagree	Approved
2017 (merger with spectrum transfer)	Velatel	OLO	Disagree	Approved
2017 (merger with spectrum transfer)	Cable Vision	OLO	Disagree	Approved
2018 (merger with spectrum transfer)	OLO	America Móvil	Disagree	Not Approved
2018 (merger with spectrum transfer)	TVS Wireless	America Móvil	Disagree	Approved

Source: Information provided by OSIPTEL, 2018.

Customer protection functions

User protection policy[2] is led by Protection and User Services department (*Gerencia de Protección y Servicio al Usuario*, GPSU). The GPSU employs 80 per cent its staff to deal with face-to-face interactions with consumers, and is primarily oriented towards complaint resolution. This is supported by three offices in Lima and the de-centralised offices and centres where the Decentralised Offices Department (*Gerencia de Oficinas Desconcentradas*, GOD) applies GPSU policies.

The GPSU focuses on both protecting consumers and providing services to users. Protection is through designing rules and supporting investigation of issues raised by consumers through legal and economic approaches. GPSU's approach focused on competition-related resolutions first, and resort to rule making when necessary. All regulations have a stated sanctioning regime for non-compliance (see more in the Supervision, enforcement and inspections section), with the final sanctioning being decided by the General Manager in the first instance and appealed to the Board of Directors in the second instance.

In addition to these mechanisms, the GPSU focuses on the provision of information to educate consumers. They view this as especially important in a dynamic market like telecommunications. While there is interest, behavioural analyses of consumer decision-making have yet to be completed. The mobile operators are prohibited from including clauses in their contracts that do not comply with current regulations.

The GOD is in charge of managing 23 regional offices and 8 centres across Peru. Decentralised offices are responsible for responding to any issues of concern in the locality, informing users of their rights, providing training for local enterprises, and measuring service quality in all regions. These offices also maintain close communication and contact with the local government to improve telecommunications access and service. Offices in Lima are set up close to the headquarters for each telecommunications provider to facilitate easy complaint filing by consumers.

The GOD has five people based in Lima and 113 individuals distributed across the different regional offices or centres. On average, each regional office employs five people responsible for advocacy and supervision and is managed by a chief lodged in a property rented by OSIPTEL. On the other hand, centres have been set up based on office-sharing agreements with local governments or institutions. These centres normally employ less staff members and are responsible for advocacy in the city they are located, in co-ordination with the head of the GOD.

Decentralised offices interact with the public on a daily basis. In more remote communities, regional language requirements make it difficult to interact. The GOD is testing innovative and proactive ways to reach out to these communities, including using rural and more visual presentations when providing information on user rights.

Strategic objectives and planning

OSIPTEL's vision is to achieve quality telecommunications services with empowered users within a framework of effective competition. This includes being recognised as an autonomous and innovative institution with committed and qualified staff. OSIPTEL defines three pillars upon which this vision is built: quality of services, customer care, and competition (see Figure 2.2). Their mission is to promote these pillars in a continuous, efficient and timely manner.

Figure 2.2. Vision and mission of OSIPTEL

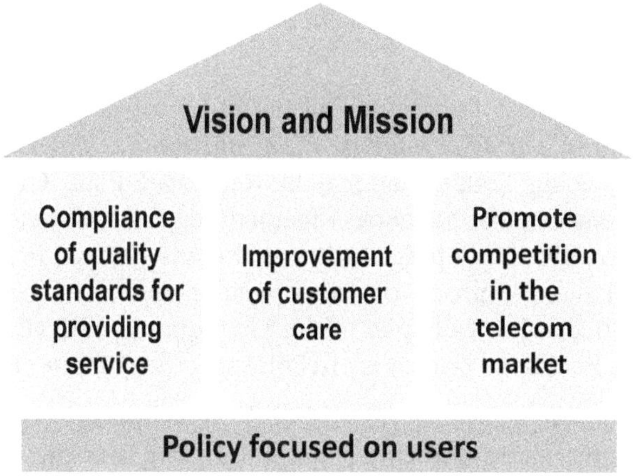

Source: Information provided by OSIPTEL, 2018.

OSIPTEL develops a five-year Strategic Institutional Plan (*Plan Estratégico Institucional*, PEI) that provides medium-term direction for accomplishing their vision and mission. The current PEI is set for the 2018-2022 period with seven strategic institutional objectives (*Objetivos Estratégicos Institucionales*, OEI) separated into core and support functions (see Table 2.7). Core objectives relate to the mission of the institution, whereas support objectives relate to the internal management and processes of OSIPTEL. The last support objective ("Implement processes for disaster risk management") is mandatory for all public bodies, as set by CEPLAN. This is an evolution from their previous PEI (2014-17), which had three objectives – one for each area of increasing competition in the market, improving satisfaction of users, and improving internal management and processes.

Table 2.7. OSIPTEL Strategic Institutional Objectives 2018-2022

Core	• Promote competition between telecommunications operators • Guarantee compliance with quality standards in telecommunications services, as established or offered by the operators • Promote appropriate attention to users by operators • Empower telecommunications service users
Support	• Consolidate OSIPTEL's reputation as a transparent and highly specialised institution • Consolidate the management model of OSIPTEL towards excellence • Implement processes for disaster risk management

Source: (OSIPTEL, 2018[1]), *Plan Estratégico Institucional 2018-22*, OSIPTEL, https://www.osiptel.gob.pe/repositorioaps/data/1/1/1/par/res025-2018-pd/res025-2018-pd_pei2018-2022.pdf (accessed 22 June 2018).

To achieve the OEIs, OSIPTEL develops Strategic Institutional Actions (*Acciones Estratégicas Institucionales*, AEI) as intermediate objectives and are reflected in the yearly operational plans (*Plan Operativo Institucional,* POI), which implements the PEI. The POI is governed by a directive and participatory plenaries are used to decide which strategic priorities to focus on in the years to come.

To achieve each AEI, it is necessary to implement a series of activities for each objective, which must also be scheduled annually in the POI. Monitoring of the POI is accomplished through the Operational Management Document, with the goal of ensuring the execution of all the activities within the framework of the AEI, since their achievement guarantees also the achievement of the strategic objectives and measured by indicators.

The process and methodology for developing the PEI are established by National Centre for Strategic Planning (*Centro Nacional de Planeamiento estratégico,* CEPLAN), who is responsible for overseeing Peru's National Development Plan. CEPLAN co-ordinates with OSIPTEL and ensures that the correct methodology is followed. In 2017, CEPLAN issued a new directive for developing institutional plans that requires bodies to provide more information relating to impacts on the population as well as geographic effects, i.e. urban versus rural affects. For example, CEPLAN requires OSIPTEL to justify how the National Fibre Optic Backbone project is affecting specific communities and individuals.

The Planning and Budget department (*Gerencia de Planeamiento y Presupuesto*, GPP) of OSIPTEL is responsible for co-ordinating and drafting the strategic objectives, which are developed in line with the main objectives, mission, and vision of the organisation and are presented to the President and the Board of Directors for approval. The GPP co-ordinates via participatory plenaries with technical staff from each department, senior management, and stakeholders that are often consulted at a later stage. Each department has a planning officer in charge of constructing indicators linked to a specific objective while technical staffs provide a diagnosis of the market situation and institutional management. Stakeholders include the PCM, related ministries, and selected regulated entities and consumers. An external consultant, selected by public competition and with knowledge of CEPLAN's methodology, ensures that the processes are respected and conducts the interviews with selected stakeholders. Members of the Board of Directors are invited to attend plenary sessions, and review the final version of the PEI or POI after approval from the President of the Board.

A technical team is also created to support the PEI and POI process. Managers from each department designate two staff members to sit on this team and accompany the entire planning process. To involve the largest number of personnel, questionnaires are sent electronically to gather opinions and contributions. During each stage of the process, workshops are held with the technical team, plenary sessions, managers of each department, the President of the Board and the General Manager. Decisions are made through a consensus format, with final approval by the President.

An annual review of the POI was introduced in 2013, but has not been formally institutionalised. Changes can be made each year to goals or specific indicators, but not to high-level objectives. Modifications are considered to be rare, as it would need to be clearly justified. The PEI and POI are displayed on the OSIPTEL website.

Communications

OSIPTEL enhances their transparency through a well-developed communications strategy that is implemented through a yearly strategic plan. Communications is directed towards the Congress, executive bodies, industry, industry associations, user associations, users and the media. However, the regulator is not required to present or discuss their annual report (discussed more in the Output and outcome section) with Congress for increased scrutiny. The communications department makes use of:

- Newsletters to industry and Congress;
- Blog oriented towards academic circles to gain support for a common interpretation of issues;
- Social media accounts, such as Twitter (84 000 followers) and Facebook (170 000 likes) designed for disseminating quick information, as well as LinkedIn (7 000 followers) to connect with professional actors, such as civil servants; and,
- Position papers periodically released on specific themes of concern.

In 2016, the regulator also invested in increased visibility in media, resulting in a doubling of OSIPTEL media appearances from 2015 to 2016 (from 2 831 to 3 626).

Consumers are making use of the social media channels to direct feedback and comments about their services to OSIPTEL, which are often responded to by officials in OSIPTEL. This is occurring in an ad hoc manner and not in association with a formal stakeholder engagement effort leveraging social media to expand outreach.

The Communications Department is also working with the Protection and Users Services Department to improve the way information is provided to consumers to enable better decision making. They are also developing a mobile-based tool to allow people to report problems with service.

The Communications department is creating a monitoring system for results and impact of its different communications mechanisms.

Independence

Article 2 of the LMOR establishes OSIPTEL as a regulatory body with administrative, functional, technical, economic, and financial autonomy. Article 10 of the General Regulations of OSIPTEL[3] further establish the autonomy principle whereby OSIPTEL is not subject to the mandate of other bodies or entities of the state, but actions are strictly subject to the applicable legal regulations and must be supported by technical studies.

The General Regulations highlight other principles that aim to support the independence of OSIPTEL. Article 7 establishes the transparency principle, which requires OSIPTEL to present their criteria for decisions and publish drafts for public consultation. Article 9 establishes an impartiality principle, which requires OSIPTEL to weigh fairness and impartiality with adherence to the relevant norms and interests of both operators and users. Finally, article 5 highlights the principle of non-discrimination that guarantees equal treatment of all operators by OSIPTEL.

In June 2018, the Commission for the Defense of Consumers and Public Services Regulatory Bodies (*Comisión de Defensa del Consumidor y Organismos Reguladores de los Servicios Publicos*, CODECO) of Congress discussed and passed a draft law to enhance aspects of institutional independence for economic regulators in Peru. The draft, which was based in part on OECD research, included measures to strengthen the regulators' administrative, functional, technical, economic and financial autonomy as well as their accountability mechanisms. As of November 2018 the draft law has not been proposed for discussion in Plenary.

Input

The LMOR grants all independent regulators with an independent source of funding based on regulatory contributions levied on the incomes of companies and entities that are under the scope of its jurisdiction.[4] Additional revenue can be collected from (OECD, 2016[2]):

- Payments from administrative procedures enlisted in their Single Text of Administrative Processes (*Texto Único de Procedimientos Administrativos*, TUPA);
- Donations, contributions, or transfers;
- International persons;
- Interests or late fees derived from the regulatory contribution;
- Financial interests generated through own resources; or
- Sources from fines.

The income of the regulator has decreased over the last years with reported industry income. While privately collected, these are considered public funds and thus enable the Congress and executive power to enact directives over how these are used, including requirements to pay into national development funds. Furthermore, a recently-introduced budget law has required non-executed budgets to be forwarded to the Treasury each year.

OSIPTEL is well-known for their highly technical staff. Like many regulators, they identify issues with competitive salaries vis-a-vis the private sector. A dual labour regime and pay freeze since 2006 may create adverse incentives for current and future staff.

Training programmes and benefit packages have been developed to help attract and retain staff, which has been successful.

Financial resources

The contribution rate collected from regulated entities is approved by the Council of Ministers through a Supreme Decree subscribed by the President of the Council of Ministers and MEF. This cannot exceed one per cent of the total annual income of regulated firms after taxes of each firm, minus GST and MPT. Supreme Decree No. 012-2002-PCM set the contribution rate at 0.5% in 2002 and has remained at that level since. The steady-state of the contribution rate at 0.5% indicates that financial resources are determined *ex ante* rather than determined in accordance with a cost recovery principle that is re-evaluated on a regular basis.

Table 2.8. provides an overview of OSIPTEL's annual budget over the last five years. Over the last three years, OSIPTEL has seen an overall decline in funds by 19% in real terms due to a decrease in industry income, in part linked to higher competition, lower prices, as well as a merger of two major companies Telefónica and Movistar in 2014. A large amount of informality, specifically in the cable TV subscription sector, also limits OSIPTEL's ability to raise funds. Finally, OSIPTEL has received new functions in line with sector evolution or new legislative texts (e.g. regulation of the National Fibre Optic Backbone) but without being granted additional resources. OSIPTEL estimates that 13 such functions have been added since 2013. Taken together, this situation has left the regulator feeling that its resources are stretched thin.

To compensate, OSIPTEL has been required to request supplemental funds to be added to their budget. These funds originate from the reserves of the regulator saved as carry over from previous years. MEF must approve access to these reserves, as well as the Modified Institutional Budget (PIM) proposed by OSIPTEL. Thanks to this mechanism, two times in four years the regulator has executed a budget higher than the initial budget received from regulatory contributions.

Any changes to contribution the rate must be made through MEF. This was attempted in 2016 by the regulator without success. The regulator has presented this request again in 2018 but the review process has been delayed due to changes in government, and the regulator has been requested tore-submit the request.

Table 2.8. OSIPTEL annual budget and execution, 2014-18

Year	2014	2015	2016	2017
Initial budget (million PEN)	79	96	82	81
Supplemental funds (million PEN)	24	8	12	12
Modified Institutional Budget (PIM, million PEN)	103	104	94	93
Execution of initial budget	120%	85%	94%	107%
Execution of Modified Institutional Budget	92%	79%	82%	93%

Notes: Initial budget is sourced from funds collected from the regulatory contributions levied to regulated entities. Supplemental funds are approved by MEF and added from the reserves of the regulator, arriving at the Modified Institutional Budget (PIM).
Source: Information provided by OSIPTEL, 2018.

Recent changes to the budget law have imposed limits on the use of this mechanism by the regulator. Since the regulator is funded solely through contributions collected directly from regulated entities, their funds are classified as "directly-collected resources" (*recursos directamente recaudados*, RDR) in contrast to "ordinary resources" (*recursos ordinarios*, RO) that are central government funds. While it is possible for OSIPTEL to receive OR funds, to date they have only ever been funded by regulatory contributions.

The national budget law previously allowed agencies with RDR funds to keep surplus funds and carry them forward to future spending, while agencies with RO funds were required to return surpluses to the Treasury each year. In 2017, the Treasury included the Law of Financial Equilibrium (*Ley de Equilibrio Financiero*) in the national budget law, which also required surplus RDR funds to be forwarded to the Treasury. This law must be renewed yearly with the national budget law. Forwarding surpluses was renewed for the 2018 Fiscal Year.[5]

Funds collected from fines and sanctions are transferred to the Telecommunications Investment Fund (FITEL), while fines associated with the taxes levied on regulated entities are kept by OSIPTEL.

Managing financial resources

In 2015, the Government of Peru, through MEF, implemented a performance budgeting system for some government entities.[6] OSIPTEL participates in this new system, which requires budgets to be aligned with the goals and objectives established by the institution in their strategic institutional plans (PEI) and operational plans (POI). This ensures that agencies consider the problems they are trying to solve and have measurable indicators of success towards solving these problems. MEF works with the various government agencies to help design better indicators by encouraging them to follow the methodology and develop indicators that show how institutional actions are leading to positive improvements in the sector and for society.

OSIPTEL utilised two budgetary processes until 2016: a three-year budget forecast and an annual budget. Both were created according to the Programming Directive, while only the annual budget required approval. For 2017 and 2018, in accordance with the shift to the performance budgeting system, the budgetary programmes changed to a single multi-annual budget that covers three years and requires the first year to be approved via the Annual Budget Law. The following two years are referential in nature and are updated yearly. MEF makes modifications in accordance with administrative simplification efforts, as well as aligning the multi-year budget with the Multiannual Macroeconomic Framework.

The multi-annual budget aligns technical analysis and decision-making on the priorities indicated in the PEI and POI. The budget includes information on goals and inputs needed to achieve these goals, broken down according to the various departments in the regulator. This requires activities, tasks and sub-tasks to be developed, followed by human and material resources being estimated. Yearly updates are submitted to MEF and Congress with details on how it will achieve its intended goals. This is then implemented through the annual budget. The goal of this process is to ensure the entity has sufficient resources for the fulfilment of its goals and objectives.

The Administration and Finance Department (GAF) co-ordinates the budget process. OSIPTEL uses expected revenue to determine how much will be available to carry out operational goals set in the POI. The GAF co-ordinates with the different internal departments, who establish the amount of budget they require to meet the goals assigned to them within a set period of time. The GAF collects and filters these demands according to the resources available and priorities identified for the upcoming year, and then presents to the President of the Board for approval.

The budget process is co-ordinated with the national government through a digital system linked with MEF that is used by all relevant government agencies. The GAF uploads the information to the Integrated System of Financial Administration (SIAF)[7] and to the Integrated Administration System (SAI).[8] Managers of each department carry out reviews of their budgetary balances through the SAI System. The GAF is responsible for updating manually the information that is not automatically interfaced with the SIAF system.

Budgetary allocations are overseen by the PCM, which have decision over some administrative allocations, including travel policies and public information campaigns.

Human resources

OSIPTEL employs 400 staff as of August 2018, of which 80% of professional staff hired are economists, engineers, or lawyers. A full breakdown of staff by occupation can be found in Table 2.9. , while a breakdown of senior and technical staff by department can be found in Table 2.10.

Table 2.9. Staff by category, 2018

Category	Female	Male
Senior management (Chairperson, manager, and advisors)	9	11
Technical staff	130	152
Support staff	64	34
TOTAL	203	197

Source: Information provided by OSIPTEL, 2018.

Table 2.10. OSIPTEL staff by department, 2018

Department	2014	2015	2016	2017	2018
Dispute resolution and appeals	37	36	39	37	35
Decentralised offices	75	76	71	66	45
Enforcement and supervision	79	76	67	53	66
Administration and finance	31	31	28	32	32
Regulatory policies and competition	44	44	44	45	38
Protection and user service	29	28	26	25	27
Information Technology, Communications and Statistics	13	13	12	12	12
Planning and budget	10	10	9	10	11
Corporate Communications	8	9	8	8	6
Legal advice	10	9	10	8	9
General Management	9	8	7	7	8
Public Prosecution	5	5	5	5	6
Presidency of the Board	3	2	2	2	3
Internal audit office	6	5	7	4	4
Support staff	67	71	61	99	98
Total workforce	426	423	396	413	400

Note: All categories of staff other than support staff are considered professional staff.
Source: Information provided by OSIPTEL, 2018.

Recruitment

The President of the Board is appointed for a five-year term by the Presidency of the Council of Ministers. The General Manager reports directly to the President of the Board. Some senior management positions are appointed by the President of the Board without term limits as "*puestos de confianza*" or "trusted positions". These positions include the General Manager, Administration and Finance Manager, Corporate Communications, Legal Advisor, Advisor to the President and Secretariat of the Board. These trusted positions can be dismissed by the President at any time. The new SERVIR labour regime (see more below) being implemented limits *puestos de confianzas* to 5% of total staff. While SERVIR is not fully implemented, Supreme Decree 084-2016-PCM establishes that the 5% rule is in full effect until the implementation of SERVIR. OSIPTEL currently only has 1.5% of staff as *puestos de confianzas*.

The remaining senior management positions have indeterminate term limits after undergoing a regular recruitment process and appointed by the President of the Board. An organisational realignment currently underway will convert the position of Head of Human Resources, which is currently a position under the Administration and Finance Manager, into a senior management position to further increase and improve HR management policies and practices.

The regular recruitment process is based on a skills model that considers both institutional and personal skills required for the position. OSIPTEL aims to recruit new employees that fit both the technical needs of the agency and are able to adapt to its institutional culture. The model identifies these skills and classifies them according to professional and functional categories (see Figure 2.3). The skills model is also used as a management tool for training and performance review.

Figure 2.3. OSIPTEL recruitment skills model

No.	COMPETENCE MATRIX osiptel	Call centre analysts / promoter - counsellor / call centre counsellors*	Call centre supervisors	Assistants and secretaries	Professionals	Chief coordinators	Sub-Managers	Managers
	INSTITUTIONAL COMPETENCIES							
1	EXCELLENCE	C	B	C	C	B	A	A
2	INTEGRITY	C	B	C	B	B	A	A
3	INNOVATION AND ANALYTIC THINKING	C	B	C	C	B	A	A
	SPECIFIC COMPETENCIES							
1	LEADERSHIP AND EFFECTIVE COMMUNICATION	C	B	C	C	B	A	A
2	PLANNING AND ORGANISATION	C	B	C	B	B	A	A
5	COMMITMENT AND TEAMWORK	C	B	C	C	B	A	A

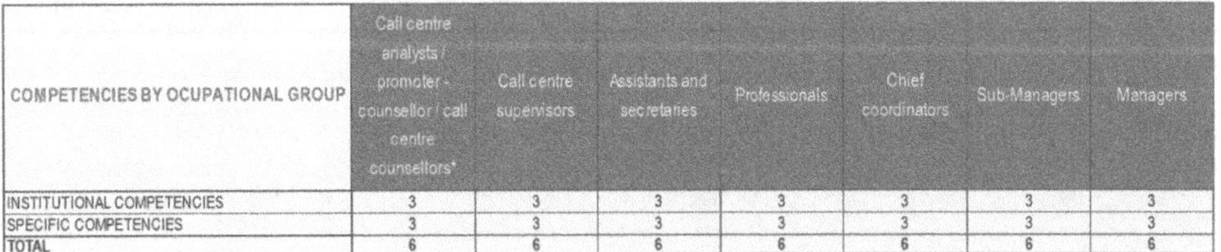

COMPETENCIES BY OCUPATIONAL GROUP	Call centre analysts / promoter - counsellor / call centre counsellors*	Call centre supervisors	Assistants and secretaries	Professionals	Chief coordinators	Sub-Managers	Managers
INSTITUTIONAL COMPETENCIES	3	3	3	3	3	3	3
SPECIFIC COMPETENCIES	3	3	3	3	3	3	3
TOTAL	6	6	6	6	6	6	6

Competency matrix

No.	Competence	Cultural vision	References
		Institutional competencies	
1	Excellence	Competitive	Go the extra mile
2	Integrity	Competitive	Probity and ethical behaviour
3	Innovation and analytical thinking	Innovation / Competitive	Initiative and new tools / Accomplish objectives
		Specific competencies	
1	Leadership and effective communication	Collaborative	Facilitate and guide / build trust between people
2	Planning and organisation	Competitive	Facilitate processes and tasks
3	Commitment and teamwork	Innovative / Collaborative	Stimulate initiative / promote teamwork

* Staff that works directly with users (on-site and by phone).
Source: Information provided by OSIPTEL, 2018.

The results of each stage are published in OSIPTEL's website. The hiring manager sends a report based on the results, which recommends hiring the candidate that obtained the highest score, to the general manager, who then takes the final decision.

OSIPTEL has an Organisation and Functions Manual, which outlines the main functions and responsibilities of the different positions within the organisation and describes the professional profile required for each position. The executive cannot nominate preferred candidates or overturn OSIPTEL's decisions.

Recruited staff members are considered as civil servants and therefore follow the rules outlined by National Civil Service Authority (SERVIR). Two employment regimes are used by regulatory authorities. The first is the Law 728 regime, which is a private regime not commonly offered in public entities (which normally follow Law 276 regime). Law 728 offers an open-ended contract term with full benefits. The number of positions is fixed, meaning that recruitments under the 728 regime can only be made when a 728 position has been vacated. Moreover, OSIPTEL must inform the Minister of Economy and Finance when hiring a new position under 728, which can cause a delay in the hiring process.

The remaining staff members are under the Law 1057 regime for "Administrative Service Contracting" (*Contratos Administrativos de Servicios,* CAS), which is a public sector regime that offers non-permanent employment on a fixed-term six-month contract that can be renewed without limit. Contracts in the last six-months of the year must end in December and renewed in January. CAS also offers less employment benefits, such as insurance or pensions, in contrast to the 728 regime. This may reduce the competitiveness of contracts offered in OSIPTEL compared to the private sector.

As of August 2018, 280 staff members are employed under Law 728, 200 under CAS.

A new labour regime introduced by SERVIR in 2013 merges both categories into one. Migration to the new regime is optional for staff under Law 728, but mandatory for staff under Law 1057. In either case, it will be necessary for the staff member to re-compete for their job in order to join the new regime.

The transition to the new SERVIR labour regime also modifies the regulations governing senior management. For example, senior managers will need to go through the formal recruitment process and all dismissals shall require proper justification, such as failing to accomplish individual goals. Term limits will also be introduced for all senior managers, which will be for three years and can be renewed for another two terms. After three terms, the official must leave the organisation. The 2016 OECD Public Governance Review of Peru, conducting as part of the OECD Country Programme for Peru, assessed, amongst other topics, the management of Peru's professional civil service and public administration reform agenda through the SERVIR law (see Box 2.2).

Box 2.2. OECD Public Governance Review of Peru: Integrated Governance for Inclusive Growth

Chapter 5. Building a stable and professional civil service in Peru

Peru's civil servants are currently under multiple labour regimes and complex employment regulations. This translates into a public labour system highly difficult to manage. For example, over 2 000 government agencies established over 500 public employment regulations and over 400 different wage criteria.

In 2013, the Peruvian government issued the new Civil Service Law (30057) for implementing an ambitious civil service reform. The law has an implementation horizon of six years and SERVIR is charged with overseeing this implementation.

The purpose of the Civil Service Law is to establish a single and exclusive scheme for civil servants at national, regional and local levels. A new pay system will be implemented for those in the new regime, with the intent to improve transparency and equity across public entities. In addition, it articulates a strategic policy rationale for the civil service reform, emphasising merit and professionalism.

The new Civil Service Law was designed based on best practice across OECD countries, and, once implemented, is expected to create a lasting impact by significantly improving the organisation, capacity, professionalism and stability of the civil service.

Nonetheless, the transition to the new regime will likely take much longer as the transition is not automatic. Civil servants can choose between transitioning to the new regime and remaining in their previous regime. Furthermore, existing civil servants will need to apply to posts in the new regime and go through a competitive process to be appointed. If they are not successful, they remain in their old post, under the old regime.

Source: (OECD, 2016[3]), *OECD Public Governance Reviews: Peru: Integrated Governance for Inclusive Growth*, OECD Public Governance Reviews, OECD Publishing, Paris, http://dx.doi.org/10.1787/9789264265172-en.

OSIPTEL has also recently developed a succession plan that identifies critical positions and potential successors, which have been used to provide more targeted training to potential successors. Succession plans developed for 12 key positions (all management) and 17 critical positions. The Administration and Finance Department identifies and evaluates successors, and then finally builds a succession map.

Remuneration

Staff members of OSIPTEL are remunerated according to limits ascribed by Supreme Decree No. 172-2013-EF and endorsed by the Chairman of the Council of Ministers and the Minister of Economy and Finances.[9] The salaries are not indexed to inflation (see Table 2.11), and OSIPTEL has no flexibility setting salaries outside of these bands.

Staff remuneration is set in accordance with their governing Laws. Both the labour and remuneration guidelines are different and independent from that of public servants in ministries and other public entities. Law 728 allows OSIPTEL to have more flexibility regarding promotions and career prospections. It also establishes salary bands higher than those considered under Law 276 for public officials.

Changes to salary bands under Law 728 must be approved by Supreme Decree, while changes to salaries under Law 1057 can happen only when an employee re-applies for a new contract. Salary bands are not indexed to inflation. The last modification to Law 728 was made in 2013.[10] All senior managers are currently remunerated at their respective maximum pay bands, which means that there have been no recent adjustments made with their salaries to meet current market conditions and compete with industry for new talent.

In partial response, the government promulgated Supreme Decree No. 024-2018-EF in 2018, raising the President of the Board of Directors salary to PEN 28 000 (USD 8 400, approximately) to be more competitive with industry.

Table 2.11. Remuneration scales at regulatory agencies in Peru (in PEN)

Job category	Minimum monthly salary	Maximum monthly salary
President	28 000	28 000
General Manager	15 600	15 600
Director, associate director or advisor	14 000	15 600
Professional I	10 700	14 900
Professional II	7 000	11 500
Professional III	5 100	10 400
Analyst	3 400	5 700
Assistant	1 900	2 500

Note: By Supreme Decree No. 172-2013-EF of 15 July 2013 and Supreme Decree No. 024-2018-EF of 9 February 2018 (for the President of the Board).
Source: Information provided by OSIPTEL, 2018.

Talent retention and training

OSIPTEL has developed a talent retention system that offers a suite of key benefit plans to attract and retain staff. A key component is an insurance plan that extends insurance to the official's dependents and parents, but is only available for staff employed under Law 728. Given these efforts, OSIPTEL has been ranked in the 2015 Great Place to Work list (El Comercio, 2015[4]) and experienced a staff turnover rate of 9.13% in 2017 compared to 18% across the Peruvian economy (see Figure 2.4.).

The regulator has recently created a gender equality commission to determine how it can attract more women into its workforce. OSIPTEL has already enacted some flexibility measures for women, including an extra week of maternity leave (in addition to the 98 days mandated by Peruvian law), as well as other more generally family-friendly policies half-days off for birthdays of children, and time off to tend to sick children.

Figure 2.4. Staff turnover rate at OSIPTEL, 2012-17

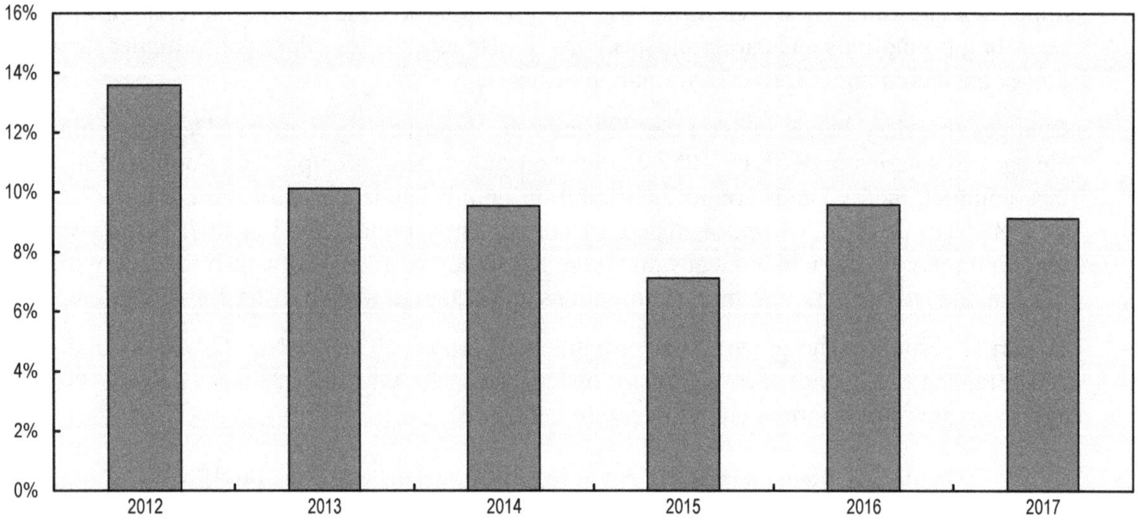

16%
14%
12%
10%
8%
6%
4%
2%
0%
2012 2013 2014 2015 2016 2017

Source: Information provided by OSIPTEL, 2018.

OSIPTEL also offers a training programme designed to fulfil the specific needs of each department, including both upgrading technical skills and covering soft-skill gaps. This program is designed in collaboration with each head of department making sure that every need is taken into consideration. The programme is tied to the performance assessment system, as it seeks to offer training related to gaps identified in the performance evaluation. The Human Resources Office inside the GAF executes at least 90% of the training activities.

The success of the training programme is measured in two ways. First, the programme requires the individual to have an average grade of 14 out of 20 in a given course for it to be considered beneficial and for the staff to achieve this grade in 80% of their training activities. Second, OSIPTEL evaluates staff performance after receiving training and the staff is expected to improve his or her performance within a year by at least 5%.

Public service training programmes as under the scope of SERVIR, as they are the national civil service authority. The new SERVIR labour regime will also contain regulations for training programmes; however, these regulations will only come into effect when the SERVIR labour regime is implemented. In the meantime, SERVIR's regulation have influenced OSIPTEL's training programme. First, OSIPTEL cannot provide further training courses until they are formally part of the new labour regime. Second, the new labour regime specifies some restrictions and commitments that the beneficiaries have to assume to be able to participate, including:

- **Type of training**: Until 2014, OSIPTEL could provide their employees with financial aid for master's degrees or PhDs. This is no longer possible due to SERVIR regulation, which dictates that the beneficiary cannot receive a degree or title from the training provided. When OSIPTEL officially implements the new SERVIR labour regime, the regulations contained in the regime will come into force and govern types of training programmes that can be offered.

- **Beneficiary Commitments**: When an employee participates in the training programme, according to SERVIR regulation, they have to assume two commitments. First, they agree to reimburse OSIPTEL the money invested in their education in case they fail the class provided. This amount is calculated according to direct costs, indirect costs and, in case the class was imparted during working hours, the equivalent to the hours they did not work according to their salary. Direct costs refer to the cost of the class itself and indirect costs refer to coffee breaks, renting of the space needed to impart the class or any other expense related to it. Second, they have to agree to keep working in the institution for a determined period of time after receiving training. The amount of time is defined by (see Table 2.12).

Table 2.12. SERVIR post-training employment requirements (in USD)

Cost of Training	Time the beneficiary has to keep working for OSIPTEL
Up to $420	Double the time the training lasted + 30 days
Between $420 and $840	Double the time the training lasted + 60 days
Between $840 and $1 258	Double the time the training lasted + 120 days
Between $1 258 and $2 515	Double the time the training lasted + 180 days
Over $2 515	Double the time the training lasted + 240 days

Source: Information provided by OSIPTEL, 2018.

Performance assessment

OSIPTEL has developed a performance assessment framework that is tied to a talent development model and talent retention system. It aims to offer staff tailored advice on career development and also provide incentives and training to fulfil technical gaps.

The performance assessment framework is linked to a competency model that defines specific skills needed to achieve OSIPTEL's strategic goals. This competency model is used to hire new staff and also evaluate current staff performance. In 2018, OSIPTEL began linking the performance assessment system with the POI to ensure tasks assigned to departments or persons correlates to objectives needing to be achieved within a given time frame.

Individual evaluations are conducted together with the staff's managers and are based on identifying and measuring both the skills and goals of the employee. Skills evaluation identifies competency gaps according to each position while goals evaluation allows staffs to set, discuss, and measure intended goals. These evaluations are then used to help managers formulate training plans and identify the skills that need to be improved or help staffs identify other suitable positions within the agency.

Since 2011, performance evaluations have been conducted via an online platform. In 2015, the system was updated in two ways. First, the process was upgraded from a 180-degree evaluation to a 270-degree evaluation, which means that employees are not the only ones evaluated in the process, but employees are also encouraged to evaluate their managers, sub-managers and chiefs. Second, a new performance evaluation model was created to allow for a more objective evaluation of skills and goals.

Given existing remuneration restrictions, well-performing employees are not rewarded for their accomplishments with any financial incentives. As an alternative, OSIPTEL holds an internal acknowledgement programme and well-performing employees are given half-day off as compensation.

To measure institutional performance, OSIPTEL conducts an Internal Customer Satisfaction Survey (ESCI) to gather opinions on the satisfaction of services provided in the different areas, and gather proposals to improve internal management and strengthen inter-agency communication. The survey gathers information on outcome (level of compliance with the services received), opportunity for attention (promptness of response and punctuality), and personal attitude (treatment, willingness, and friendliness).

Process

OSIPTEL is headed by a Board of Directors and President of the Board, who make a wide variety of executive decisions. Its General Management conducts the technical functions in regards to regulation, user protection, and supervision, and is supported by horizontal functions carried out by various departments.

OSIPTEL uses regulatory quality tools to varying degrees, such as RIA, stakeholder engagement and *ex post* evaluation to improve their decision-making process.

Decision making and governance structure

The Board of Directors is the highest authority in the regulatory agency and carries out mostly executive decision-making functions. The Board is composed of five members – four who are part-time and one who is full time and serves as the President of the Board. The current composition of the Board is two lawyers, two engineers, and one economist. Members hold office for five years on staggered terms (one appointment per year)[11] and can be re-appointed to serve one additional term (see Box 2.3). However, in 2018, three board positions are expiring and will be replaced concurrently, which may pose a risk to continuity in decision making (see Table 2.13). Supreme Decree No. 082-2018-PCM was issued by the PCM, extending their mandates once by 90 days. At time of writing new members had yet to be appointed and the Board was operating with only two active members, including the President.

Table 2.13. Ten-year history of OSIPTEL board members

Member	Role	Profession	Start date	End date
Rafael Eduardo Muente Schwartz	President	Lawyer	2017	2022
Jesús Eduardo Guillén Marroquín	Board member	Economist (PhD)	2017	2021
Manuel Ángel Cipriano Pirgo	Board member	Lawyer	2013	2018[1]
Jesús Otto Villanueva Napurí	Board member	Mechanical and electrical engineer	2013	2018[2]
Víctor Jesús Revilla Calvo	Board Member	Civil engineer	2015	2018[3]
Gonzalo Martín Ruiz Díaz	President	Economist (PhD)	2012	2017[4]
Humberto Eduardo Zolezzi Chacón	Board member	Electrical engineer	2011	2016[5]
Manuel Ángel Cipriano Pirgo	Board member	Lawyer	2013	2013[6]
Víctor Jesús Revilla Calvo	Board member	Civil engineer	2010	2013[7]
Carlos Daniel Durand Chahud	Board member	Systems engineer	2010	2011

Notes: 1., 2., & 3. Received 90 day extension according to Supreme Decree No. 072-2018-PCM; 4., 5., 6. & 7. stayed 60 calendar days after the end of their terms, in accordance with provisions in article 7 of the Regulations of the Framework Law, approved by Supreme Decree No. 042-2005-PCM.
Source: Information provided by OSIPTEL, 2018.

In the event that a board member leaves before the end of their term, the new member is only appointed for the remaining amount of time. Vacancies must be filled within 30 days of the expiration of a member's term, though can be exceptionally extended by 60 days through Supreme Decree. This is currently in force for the three board members leaving in 2018 due to delays in the nomination procedure of new members.

The Board is responsible for setting the strategic direction, developing policy, and setting a clear process for executing the mandate of the organisation. They exert functions related to promoting competition and consumer protection, as well as issue non-binding technical opinions when requested by the executive or congress. The Board also designates and removes members of the appellate bodies and acts as a sanction function in the second instance.

Box 2.3. Board of directors selection process

Criteria for selection as a Board member are:

- Be a professional with no less than ten (10) years of practice;
- Have recognised professional solvency and suitability, by way of no less than three years of experience in a position of executive management, with understanding of the decision making in public or private companies; or five years of experience in matters related to the competence of the regulatory body; and;
- Complete studies at the master's level in subjects related to the competence of the regulatory body.

All members of the Board are selected by:

- A selection committee composed of one member proposed by the PCM, one member proposed by Indecopi, one member proposed by MEF and one member proposed by the sectorial ministry related to regulator activities;
- The President of the Council of Ministers, who submits to the President of the Republic the final list of selected candidates; and
- The President of the Republic, who appoints the member of the Board by Supreme Resolution, which will be endorsed by the President of the Council of Ministers, the Minister of Economy and Finance and the sectorial ministry related to the regulator activities.

Board Members can be dismissed due to legal impediments following the appointment, unjustified absences from two consecutive sessions unless authorised, or in the case of serious misconduct. A one-year restriction on post-employment for employees of the regulator is applied to board members, as it is for staffs.

Source: Law No. 27332; Supreme Decree 103-2012-PCM; Supreme Decree No. 014-2008-PCM; (OECD, 2016[2]), *Regulatory Policy in Peru: Assembling the Framework for Regulatory Quality*, OECD Reviews of Regulatory Reform, OECD Publishing, Paris, http://dx.doi.org/10.1787/9789264260054-en.

To maintain the independence of the Board, the only interaction between the Board and staff of the regulator is intended to be through Board sessions and with respect to the issues being addressed in those sessions. The decision making process is as follows:

- Departments of the General Management are responsible for proposing and sustaining specific sectoral issues entered into the agenda of the Board session, which must have the approval of the General Manager.

- The topics proposed in the agenda, together with its supporting documents, are made available to the members of the Board at least two days prior to the session.
- During the session, if necessary, those responsible for the proposed topic briefly explain the content of the proposal and answer the questions of the members of the Board.
- The Board adopts its decisions in the session.

The President of the Board is the only member with a full time position with the regulator. The remaining four members are remunerated PEN 3 000 (approximately USD 900) per month, with the requirement to attend two meetings each month and can be requested to meet additionally under extraordinary circumstances by the President of the Board or a majority of its members. They are not provided additional remuneration on these occasions. This structure can limit Board members' ability to fully examine issues, especially when the Board has to consider new, non-routine, or complex topics. There are no advisor positions available to members of the Board other than the President. Changes to remuneration rules require an amendment to the Law.

Quorum for meetings is set at half of the members being present and requires the attendance of the President or Vice-President of the Board. Votes are determined by a simple majority of the members attending. The agenda and minutes of Board meetings are posted on the OSIPTEL website.

President of the Board of Directors

The Board of Directors is represented on a full-time basis by the President of the Board, who performs the executive functions of the regulator. The President is responsible for setting the strategic direction and functions of the Board, exerts executive and administrative functions, and reports on behalf of the regulator to the PCM and MEF.

The President is selected through a public contest. A selection committee composed of two members from the PCM, one member proposed by MEF and one by the MTC proposes a list of applicants to the President of the Council of Ministers, who submits to the President of the Republic the proposed selected candidate. The President of the Board of Directors is then appointed via a Supreme Decree signed by the President of the Republic and endorsed by the President of the Council of Ministers.

The President presides over the Board, implements the decisions of the Board, and represents OSIPTEL before public authorities and national or foreign institutions. The President also designates or removes the General Manager and approves, at the proposal of the General Manager, the hiring, promotion, suspension, or removal of line managers and management-level officials. Some managers are directly appointed by the President as special positions or "*puestos de confianza*". Finally, the President approves the institutional budget, balance sheets and financial statements as well as the Institutional Management Plan and administrative policies.

The President transmits the Board's strategic directions via weekly meetings with the General Manager and senior management. The President is supported by two advisors that work directly for the office.

General Manager

The General Manager is responsible for the legal, administrative, and judicial responsibilities of OSIPTEL. Appointed by the President at-will and without open recruitment, the General Manager is responsible for legal, administrative, and judicial responsibilities of OSIPTEL and plans, organises, manages, executes and supervises the administrative, operational, economic and financial activities of OSIPTEL. The General Manager also prepares draft annual reports, budgets and makes senior management recruitment decisions, which are approved for decision by the President.

The General Manager also attends sessions of the Board, but does not have a voting function. For discussions pertaining to appeals of decisions made by the General Management, the General Manager must withdraw from the session.

The General Manager is supported by one advisor, but has the authority to request support from staff in various departments. Consultants can also be hired under the direction of the General Manager and by the responsible department, following national procurement rules. The General Manager can also convene the managers of the various departments to work on special projects.

Together, the President of the Board and the General Manager chair a weekly meeting with OSIPTEL senior management.

Internal organisation

OSIPTEL is organised into five sections (see Figure 2.5 for full organigram):

- **Strategic bodies:** Board of Directors, President of the Board and the General Manager, described above.
- **Line bodies:** Responsible for developing regulations, conducting supervisions and protecting users according to their specific duties.
- **Advisory bodies:** Responsible for developing and proposing advice and initiatives to the General Manager on issues related to Legal Advisory Department, Planning and Budget Department, and Corporate Communications.
- **Support bodies:** Provide the General Management with Administration and Finance Department, and IT services.
- **Dispute resolution bodies:** Responsible for handling user complaints and disputes between companies, and is supported by a technical secretariat. It is preferred to disband the Arbitration Centre due to enterprises preferring to bring their cases via other avenues. However, this requires a change in law.

Most departments report to the General Manager, with the exception of the Technical Secretariat, Internal Control, and the Public Prosecutor who report directly to the President of the Board.

The Institutional Control Body (OCI) is part of the National Control System and is responsible for ensuring compliance with the annual plans and programmes, and external governmental control on behalf of the Comptroller General of the Republic of Peru. The Public Prosecutor's Office is in charge of the legal defence of OSIPTEL's interests. It has autonomy to exercise its functions and must comply with the principles of the State Legal Defense System.

The Planning and Budget Department (GPP) plays a co-ordinating role within OSIPTEL, as it is responsible for gathering information obtained from internal surveys and reviews, which are reported to the Managers Committee and the President of the Board. The final report is used to improve performance in each department, notably in terms of outcomes, attention and personnel attitude. Managers of each department are requested to submit comments, decisions or recommendations to corresponding personnel/area, following a performance review, to improve co-ordination and collaboration with other departments.

Figure 2.5. OSIPTEL organisational structure

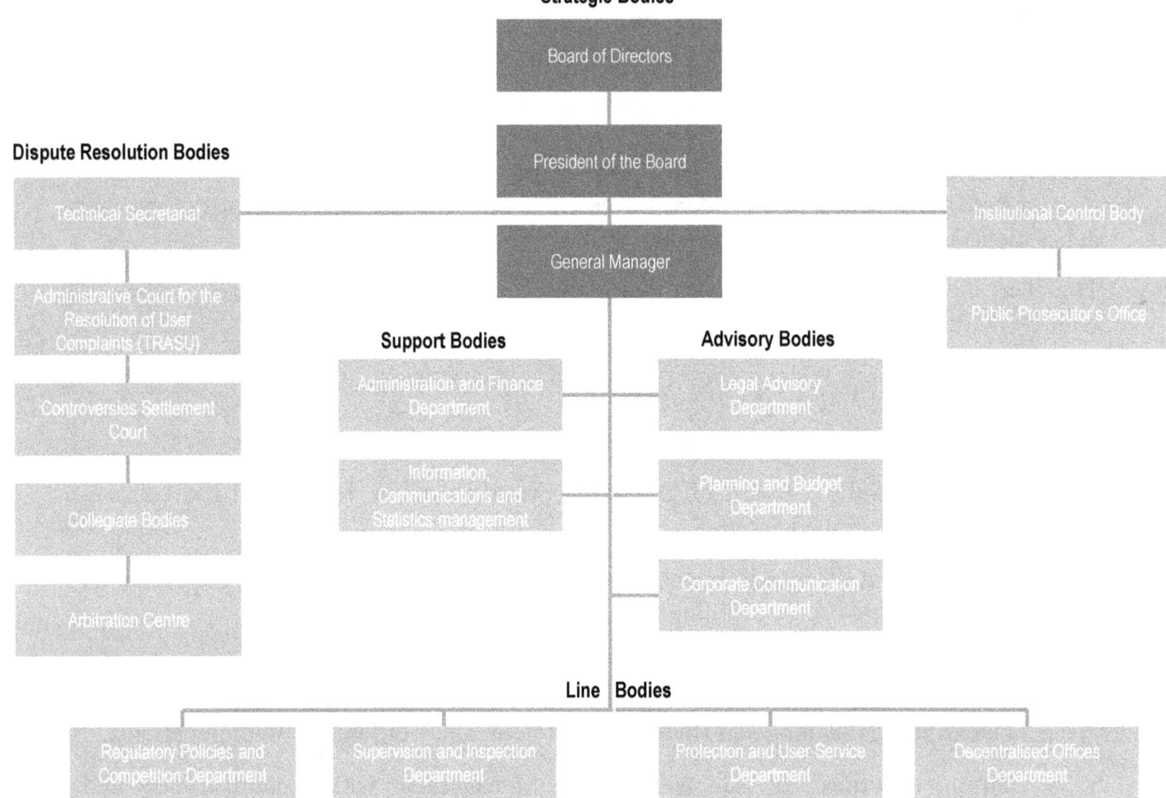

Source: Information provided by OSIPTEL, 2018.

A high priority has been placed on obtaining international certifications for management and processes, including the SGSI Certification for ISO 27001 (information security management systems) and the SGS certification for ISO 9001 (quality management systems) in 2015, which requires yearly re-certification. OSIPTEL has also been awarded the 2016 National Quality Award in the public sector category in recognition of its management model, and the 2017 Association of Good Employers (ABE) Award for Labour Social Responsibility in the category of Best Work Flexibility Program.

A formal practice has also existed since 2003 to send preliminary analyses on draft regulations to the various departments for feedback. This is normally done through a memo attached to the draft regulation. In 2017, the General Manager improved the process by encouraging departments seeking feedback to provide concrete action points, including a timeline.

Regulatory quality

In 2016, the PCM issued Law Decree No. 1310 on Regulatory Quality Assessment (RQA), with draft rulings and guidelines in July 2017. The full rulings and guidelines are expected in 2018. The RQA is a procedure to assess regulations that establish administrative procedures to identify, reduce and/or eliminate unnecessary, unjustified, disproportionate, or redundant procedures (Ministerial Resolution No. 196-PCM-2017). The rulings and guidelines apply to all public entities of the executive branch.

The Decree and support documents will require all government entities to perform RQAs on all regulations that establish administrative procedures. The Decree establishes three actions: requiring an *ex ante* assessment of impactfor new procedures, a review of the regulatory stock, and a revision to the regulatory stock every three years to reduce burdens. The decree limits this to procedural changes related to administrative processes and not for all regulatory measures.

A Multi-Sectoral Commission on Regulatory Quality (MCRQ) was also establish as a permanent body that reports to the Presidency of the Council of Ministers. The MCRQ serves to assess and validate the RQAs conducted by public entities of the executive branch according to four principles: legality, necessity, effectiveness, and proportionality. The MCRQ issues its observations and proposals for improving the measure, which is sent to the public entity for correction or acceptance and then back to the MCRQ for validation. The MCRQ can also propose the dismissal of an administrative procedure if it does not meet the principles of legality or necessity.

Prior to PCM's decision to implement the RQA, OSIPTEL has been using regulatory quality initiatives to improve decision- and policy-making. OSIPTEL is considered as the first public entity that required studies for each regulatory provision introduced and published upcoming initiatives as a way to welcome feedback and suggestions from private and public stakeholders (OSIPTEL, 2014[5]).

Independently and in parallel to the development of the PCM RQA, three regulators – Osinergmin, OSIPTEL and OSITRAN – developed manuals and guidelines for assessing the impacts of regulatory decisions. These manuals extend the scope of analysis and application of assessments to include a wider scope of regulatory decisions, and not just those affecting administrative procedures. In January 2017, OSIPTEL published a "Regulatory Quality Commitment," which sets the framework for good regulatory governance and continuous improvement of OSIPTEL's regulatory policy tools via:

- Adherence to ISO 9001 (see above)
- Mandatory use of RIA
- Publish all proceedings on the website of the regulator
- Use *Regulatory Technique Guidelines* and *Regulatory Quality Guidelines* to standardise language/structure

In March 2018, OSIPTEL issued a set of "Guidelines for Regulatory Quality" (*Lineamientos de Calidad Regulatoria*), concurrent with the release of PCM's RQA requirements. These guidelines establish a mandatory framework to strengthen the good practices of the regulatory policies undertaken by OSIPTEL in the fulfilment of its functions.[12]

OSIPTEL uses international standards to inform their performance and develop solutions. Since 2013, OSIPTEL has subscribed to Cullen International, an international benchmarking database operated out of Belgium that compares regulations of different countries in the telecommunications sector and presents details comparatively. This is used to develop new regulations according to international practices.

Regulatory impact assessments

OSIPTEL is considered as an early adopter of RIA in Peru. Prior to the release of its Guidelines for Regulatory Quality, OSIPTEL has been conducting regulatory impact assessments (RIAs) on draft regulations, but not on a mandatory or systemic basis and not released for public use. RIAs are conducted by the technical staff in all departments that propose norms or regulations and they are supported by the Legal Advisory Department (GAL) that also reviews the legal quality of the draft regulations. All RIAs drafted are overseen by the counsellor of the President of the Board, who is independent of the regulatory process. This counsellor performs this function in addition to other duties. They also have the power to block and send back inadequate RIAs before presenting to the Board.

According to the new guidelines, regulations can be assessed using a cost-benefit analysis, cost-effectiveness analysis, or multi-criteria analysis. To date, assessments conducted by OSIPTEL have used both multi-criteria analysis and cost-benefit analysis. Cost-benefit analysis should also be consistent with the proportionality principle and based on market prices.

RIAs are included in the package of documents sent to the Board for approval. A simplified version compared to the one presented to the Board is published online for the public consultation process with stakeholders. RIAs are also included in the final regulation alongside the comments matrix.

Stakeholder engagement

Public consultations are not mandatory in Peru. The only form of consultation required by law is to publish new laws and regulations in the Official Gazette, web page or other instrument at least 30 days before its entry into force, in order for public bodies to receive comments and make necessary modifications.

All economic regulators prepare a matrix of comments that assembles stakeholders' comments on a regulatory proposal. This is published together with an evaluation from the regulator on how the comments will be considered in the draft regulation (OECD, 2016[2]).

According to the LMOR, economic regulators are also required to have one or more Councils of Users that serves as a mechanism for stakeholder participation for each sector. Council members are elected for two years and can operate at the local, regional, or national level, depending on the characteristics of the market. When forming a Council, regulators publish information on a call for potential candidates, a provisional list of candidates, and a final list of elected members. Member councils can come from consumer associations, universities, professional colleges, non-profit organisations and business organisations not related with the regulated entities.

Despite this requirement, there is no active Council of Users consulted by OSIPTEL on proposed initiatives, in part due to inadequate incentive mechanisms for them to engage in meaningful exchange. Positions on the Councils are not remunerated, and the regulator does not finance the functioning in the Councils.

In 2016, OSIPTEL incorporated the requirement to conduct stakeholder engagement into their General Rules for all normative projects via the OSIPTEL website, which includes the requirement to collect opinions from the public and conduct a public hearing when necessary. Each department in charge of a norm or regulation co-ordinates the stakeholder engagement process throughout the comment period.

An informal and non-mandatory early stage consultation is sometimes conducted with external stakeholders when OSIPTEL begins the analysis of a potential draft regulation. During these consultations, OSIPTEL may ask stakeholders for information or feedback on the issue, statistics, or impact. Feedback is collected from users, enterprises, or relevant stakeholders. No formal advisory body exists, but a select group of private companies is occasionally contacted on an ad hoc basis for opinions early in the regulatory process.

During the various stages of the regulatory process, operators may request a meeting with the Board of Directors or specific working groups. A summary of the meeting, including its attendees, is posted on the OSIPTEL website. This practice appears to have been scaled back in 2018, as access has been restricted for regulated entities to discuss issues that are in the regulatory development phase. They must then wait until the public consultation period to provide their inputs into draft laws.

Changes in tariffs and interconnection charges also require public hearings. In the case of tariff regulations, public hearings must take place in three cities – one in each of the north, south and centre – and selected according to the number of people using the regulated service. Public hearings must be conducted for at least 20 days. Specific operators who may be impacted directly by the draft regulation may also be permitted extra time to provide a presentation of their opinions on the public hearings

OSIPTEL has been experimenting with innovative methods such as Facebook Live to also increase participation from user groups, as well as occasionally conducting seminars with academic audiences. The effectiveness of these methods has not yet been evaluated.

Public administration entities may participate as stakeholders in the engagement process, but their comments have no mandatory effect and are evaluated along with the comments presented by the stakeholders.

According to the Guidelines on Regulatory Quality, supporting documents must be included when a draft is published for comment to provide stakeholders with more information prior to the consultation process, such as the cost model, where applicable, in excel format. In some cases, a press release is also prepared.

The final regulation plus a matrix of consultation comments are published as one document on the OSIPTEL website. The resolution is also published in the Gazette, with a statement that all supporting information can be found on the OSIPTEL website. The matrix provides a summary of all comments received and a response from OSIPTEL explaining and justifying its decision.

When a new regulation is approved, the Communications Department releases a press release and organises interviews on main radio stations or television channels to explain and raise awareness on the new regulation. OSIPTEL also participates in different forums or seminars to provide more in-depth information on new regulations. However, due to budget constraints, large scale campaigns are used on a limited basis.

Ex post *reviews*

In accordance with the PCM RQA, economic regulators in Peru are only required to undertake stock reviews and *ex post* evaluations for regulations that add administrative procedures. In OSIPTEL, *ex post* evaluations of regulations not covered by the RQA are ad hoc and completed only for specific regulations, usually involving controversial decisions. In some cases, evaluations are indicated in some regulations through a sunset clause or are set by OSIPTEL's existing norms.

For price regulations and interconnections charges, OSIPTEL is required to evaluate the conditions of the market every four years to determine if a change is necessary.[13] OSIPTEL uses market data collected to monitor operators classified as having Significant Market Power (SMP) and make necessary modifications when failures are detected. This classification is subject to a sunset clause, which requires OSIPTEL to re-evaluate every three years to see if the operator continues to have the SMP classification. This analysis can be done every two years if the regulator has strong evidence of a significant change in market conditions or if requested by a regulated entity.

OSIPTEL also carries out periodic analyses of the telecommunications market to identify the impacts of existing or newly introduced regulations or modifications. These analyses look at main statistics, such as number/evolution of lines, penetration, traffic, market share, incomes (by market, by economic group). In addition, OSIPTEL actively monitors telecommunications enterprises offers (main plans, prices, specific characteristics) and consumers demand.

Each department within OSIPTEL is responsible for evaluating their own regulations, and are not conducted via established quantitative or qualitative criteria. Consultation with external stakeholders or the public is not used. However, OSIPTEL often receives advice from firms on an ad hoc basis requesting to remove regulations that may not be necessarily related to the regulation under review.

In accordance with the PCM RQA, OSIPTEL is reviewing its stock of regulations to determine which need to be removed or revised. This review will extend past administrative processes, as required by the RQA, and include all norms enacted by OSITPEL. The GAL is leading this process, which has compiled a list of all regulations and norms established since 1994. The Legal Department is currently requesting departments to identify regulations that need to be reviewed and set a timeline for the review. An external consultant has been hired and an ad hoc group has been created to conduct the process.[14] This group will deliver its conclusions in 2019. From 2019 to 2021, OSIPTEL will repeal, modify, or leave unchanged the regulations in accordance with the recommendations.

OSIPTEL has committed to reviewing four regulations in 2018, with one completed in the second quarter. The entire process is scheduled for completion by 2021. Some regulations will be reviewed in tandem and combined into a single consolidated text.

OSIPTEL has recently established a committee to carry on the *ex post* evaluation of norms, focusing on typifying conducts that will be subject to supervision and, eventually, sanctions. The committee is chaired by the Regulatory Policy and Competition department, and includes officials of the Supervision, Legal, and Users Protection departments as well as Technical Secretariat. The goal of the committee is to issue a norm with all sanctionable conduct, which will make OSIPTEL more predictable and facilitate more efficient supervision function.

Supervision, enforcement and inspections

Inspections are performed by the Enforcement and Supervision department (*Gerencia de Supervisión y Fiscalización*, GSF), who have an assigned staff of professionals in Lima as well as one in each of the 23 decentralised offices. The inspectors are specialised in different areas – including engineering, law, and economics – to develop a multidisciplinary approach to both inspection and the administrative procedures associated with enforcement.

Inspection plans are made yearly and programmed to visit areas that are new, have not been visited recently, or have faced infractions in the previous year. Information collected from inspection activities are transmitted from the regional offices to the Lima office for analysis.

Supervisions are conducted with the goal of compliance and prevention, which is also reinforced by the General Administration Procedure Rules that establishes the normative goal for inspections. OSIPTEL works with regulated entities using education or trainings to improve performance and contracts and to encourage resolutions before any sanction is imposed. Supervisions are carried out in three areas:

- **Quality of service**: mainly focused on the technical delivery of fixed and mobile internet and mobile voice services, which needs to meet OSIPTEL standards. A variety of indicators are measured using field tests with specialised equipment. Quality of service indicators specified in the framework of the PPP projects associated with the National Fiber Optic Backbone and coverage of spectrum auctions are also enforced by GSF under this area.
- **User rights**: focused on protecting consumers in the market, related to subscriptions and termination of service, over charges, and portability. Also, OSIPTEL supervises the Register of Stolen or Lost Cellular Phones, which was created to avoid these phones be used in the mobile networks.
- **Management**: focused on ensuring that all processes in the GSF are managed consistently, given that different inspectors will view supervisions differently.

Annual inspection plans vary according to the different areas. For Quality of Service, inspection plans are made yearly and programmed to visit areas that are new, have not been visited recently, or have faced infractions in the previous year. Information collected is transmitted from the regional offices to the Lima office for analysis. For User Rights, inspection plans are organised in accordance with the regulations that govern this area. Supervisors are usually deployed at the national level and issues are divided between recurring issues (to promote consistent behaviour change of the operating companies) and circumstantial issues (i.e. those generated from implementation or regulatory changes).

Sanctioning involves a lengthy administrative process that can take over two years to complete and involve opening three separate files. The files involve iterations of inspections and contracts for improvement with the regulated entity before sanctions are levied. When a sanction is levied, the governing regulation gives the procedure and ranges for sanctions according to three levels: light, moderate or heavy. The governing regulation gives the procedure for arriving at the amount of the sanction, which is normally in accordance with economic principles, i.e. the rate of return or revenue divided by the probability of detection.

The first instance for sanctions are handled by the line department responsible for the supervision, who forwards a proposal to the General Manager. The General Manager approves or revises the sanction to increase or decrease the amount within the bounds of the governing legislation. Second instance appeals are handled by the Board of Directors, which occurs in most cases.

Funds from sanctions are sent in their entirety to FITEL, and decisions are posted on the OSIPTEL website as part of the mandatory procedure for transparency. OSIPTEL wishes to extend this provision and public all decisions to include the case of no sanction.

Enforcement and inspections are an increasingly resource intensive activity for OSIPTEL (see Table 2.14). One inspector may be insufficient for some areas, especially those with challenging terrain that impedes access and accuracy of tests. Under Peruvian law, OSIPTEL is not allowed to hire third party companies to ease the burden on their inspectors and lawyers.

Table 2.14. Enforcements, by year

Year	Inspections	Breaches detected	Measures taken
2015	339	113	• Administrative sanctioning: 86 • Preventative: 23 • Corrective: 6
2016	259	126	• Administrative sanctioning: 117 • Corrective: 21
2017	249	99 (72 still ongoing)	• Administrative sanctioning: 76 • Preventative: 5 • Corrective: 22 • Additional supervisions: 8

Note: Data on inspections can be found at https://www.osiptel.gob.pe/documentos/registro-de-sanciones.
Source: Information provided by OSIPTEL, 2018.

In 2017, the Government modified the Administrative Procedures Rules to shift focus from compliance-based supervision to performance-based supervision. The modifications are aimed at improving performance across ministries and government agencies and diagnosing and preventing unwarranted behaviours. For example, if an enterprise has violated the rules but complies later in advance of sanctioning procedures being commenced, then the enterprise has no negative consequences and the sanctioning procedure is cancelled. If the compliance occurs after the sanctioning procedure has commenced, then a discount of the total fine is applied. In this sense, the supervision itself has not changed but the evaluation and imposition of sanctions has changed.

Appeals

OSIPTEL has four dispute resolution bodies for the telecommunications sector, supported by a technical secretariat that administers these functions, except in the case of sanctions imposed on regulated entities that involves the Board of Directors in the second instance. An overview of the role of these different bodies in dispute resolution can be found in Table 2.15. The four dispute resolution bodies are:

- Arbitration centre
- Collegiate bodies
- Controversies settlement court
- Administrative court for the resolution of user complaints (*Tribunal Administrativo de Solución de Reclamos de Usuarios*, TRASU)

Table 2.15. Map of dispute resolution pathways for regulated entities and users

Stage	Administrative issues between regulated entities	Sanctions imposed on regulated entities	User complaints	Sanctions levied by TRASU
First instance	Collegiate Bodies	Line department responsible for enforcing the regulation, approved by GM	The regulated entity	TRASU
Second instance	Controversies settlement court	Board of Directors	TRASU	Board of Directors
Final review	Contentious administrative process via Peruvian Judiciary	Contentious administrative process via Peruvian Judiciary	Contentious administrative process via Peruvian Judiciary	Contentious administrative process via Peruvian Judiciary

Notes: For administrative issues between regulated entities, the entities can voluntarily elect to use the Arbitration Centre when there is an infringement related to their contracts and there is not any violation to compulsory regulations. For consumer complaints, TRASU in the second instance can levy a sanction. When doing so, the sanction becomes a first instance decision, in which case the Board of Directors serves as the second instance arbiter.
Source: Information provided by OSIPTEL, 2018.

Two pathways exist for resolving administrative issues between regulated entities. First, the Arbitration Centre is dedicated to the resolution of disputes in the telecommunications sector through institutionally-supported arbitration and reconciliation. Companies volunteer to use the Arbitration Centre in lieu of the other administrative review bodies (i.e. Collegiate Bodies and Controversies Settlement Court), whereby one or more arbiters are selected to hear the case and make a binding decision. This also avoids an examination of infringements or violations of the law or illegal conduct by the other administrative review bodies. However, to date, only one case has been heard by the Arbitration Centre.

Second, the majority of cases between companies are resolved through the Collegiate Bodies and Controversies Settlement Court. The Collegiate Bodies hear the case in the first instance and Controversies Settlement Court in the second instance. Both bodies handle administrative issues related to free and unfair competition or subjects of interconnection, access, infrastructure sharing and tariffs.

In terms of composition, the Collegiate Bodies are composed of between three and five members appointed by the OSIPTEL Board of Directors from a preliminary list approved by the Body. In cases of free competition and unfair competition, two Permanent Collegiate Bodies can be formed for a period of three years. As of 2018, only one Permanent Collegiate Body has been formed. In the case of controversies, the Board of Directors appoints an Ad hoc Collegiate Body for each case. Members of the Controversies Settlement Court are nominated by the PCM and MEF, with one member nominated by the MTC and another by Indecopi.

User complaints are handled through a different dispute resolution pathway. In the first instance, users must launch their complaint directly with the regulated entity. If the complaint is not resolved, then the user can appeal their case in the second instance to the Administrative court for the resolution of user complaints (TRASU).[15] The process was established in 1994[16] and updated in 2015.[17] TRASU decides on the merit of the case, and can also choose to levy sanctions in accordance with infractions to established procedures or breaking of resolutions issued by TRASU. Sanctions levied by TRASU become a first instance decision, which can be appealed in the second instance to the OSIPTEL Board of

Directors who serves as the final arbiter on these sanctions. Funds from sanctions are sent in their entirety to FITEL and decisions are posted on the OSIPTEL website for transparency.

The Board of Directors of OSIPTEL nominate members of TRASU. At the time of writing, the Board implemented extraordinary rules for the organisation of TRASU in 2018 (Resolution No. 051-2018-CD/OSIPTEL) to deal with an excess workload (see Table 2.16). These extraordinary measures are to last 18 months and permit hiring extra staff to process the complaints that can be handled quickly.

Table 2.16. Organisation of TRASU before and after extraordinary measures, 2018

Original organisation of TRASU	Organisation of TRASU according to extraordinary measures
• Two collegiate chambers located in Lima, each with three people • Six uniperson chambers located in Lima • Seven uniperson chambers, one in each of the following regions of Peru: Arequipa, La Libertad, Piura, Lambayeque, Junin, Cusco and Loreto.	• Two collegiate chambers located in Lima reorganised into six uniperson chambers that focus on national-level issues, regardless of amount of money claimed • Six uniperson chambers located in Lima remain, but shift focus to national-level issues, regardless of amount of money claimed • Six new uniperson chambers in Lima that focus on national-level issues, regardless of amount of money claimed. • If deemed necessary by the President of the Board, a Transitory Collegiate Chamber can be created to solve administrative penalties

Note: The original six uniperson chambers located in Lima focus on 1) Complaints about issues during the procedure, 2) Appeals for issues that can be solved in 15 working days, or 3) Appeals on issues with claim amounts less than PEN 100.
Source: Information provided by OSIPTEL, 2018.

The excess workload was caused by an exponential rise in consumer complaints from 2015 to 2017 (see Table 2.17). This was caused, amongst other reasons, by a provision in Peruvian law that allows users to receive a holiday from paying their bills if the appeal of their complaint is still being decided. This was exacerbated by third-party services who filed complaints on behalf of users, a situation that is that is expected to change with new regulatory rules in 2018. So far, the extraordinary measures have reduced the second instance claims from approximately 43 000 in February 2018 (before the emergency rules) to 14 000 in July 2018.

Table 2.17. First and second instance complaints by users, 2015-17

Format for complaint	2015	2016	2017	2018*
In person	338 864	515 073	680 280	382 685
Written	29 817	17 939	22 808	9 936
Phone	840 846	1 438 268	2 656 667	1 090 803
Web page	64 243	162 665	286 990	133 487
Other	10	23	243	22 347
TOTAL	**1 273 780**	**2 133 958**	**3 647 026**	**1 639 258**
Second instance (on average)	31 226	59 047	159 371	14 643

Notes: OSIPTEL reports that on average, 3.5% of first instance complaints move to second instance appeals with TRASU. 2018 statistics are as of June 2018.
Source: Information provided by OSIPTEL, 2018.

Any additional appeals to the first and second instances of each body described above must be done through judicial review, which can take up to five to eight years to complete. For second instance decisions by the collegiate bodies or TRASU, a judicial review can be filed as a "contentious administrative process" under Law No. 27584. Justices have the ability to decide the case based on both the merit of the issue as well as process. Tariff decisions can also be appealed via judicial review. Judicial reviews launched by users are rare, due to the lengthy period of time it takes decide cases. Details on the decisions of OSPITEL appealed in courts can be found in Table 2.18.

Table 2.18. OSIPTEL decisions appealed in courts and outcomes

Year	Number of decisions taken	Number of decisions appealed	Status (decision upheld, rejected, ongoing)
2016	69	36	Decision upheld: 3 Rejected: 0 On-going: 33
2015	67	41	Decision upheld: 6 Rejected: 0 On-going: 35
2014	62	63	Decision upheld: 25 Rejected: 0 On-going: 38
2013	39	79	Decision upheld: 44 Rejected: 0 On-going: 35
2012	62	58	Decision upheld: 34 Rejected: 1 On-going: 22

Source: Information provided by OSIPTEL, 2018.

When an operator deems a law imposed by the Board of Directors as unconstitutional or against the existing legal frameworks, they can launch a "Popular Act" appeal in accordance with article 200 of the Political Constitution of Peru. Regulated entities can also challenge decisions that impose administrative burdens under Legislative Decree No. 1256, which approves the Law on the Prevention and Elimination of Administrative Burden.

Transparency, integrity and accountability

OSIPTEL is directly accountable to the PCM as well as Congress, but can be called upon by the MTC or other relevant government departments to provide information or opinions. Although OSIPTEL publishes an annual report on their website, there is no requirement to officially share and present this with any state entities. The PCM and MEF do require the regulator to report on certain indicators and meet reporting requirements; however, these are often fragmented.

The actions of OSIPTEL are governed by the Transparency Principle,[18] which requires regulations issued to be published in the Official Gazette, *El Peruano*, and on its website. All resolutions that create or influence mandatory administrative processes as well as those that impose sanctions relating to serious or very serious infractions must also be published in the Official Gazette.[19]

OSIPTEL makes use of their website to publish regulatory decisions, results from stakeholder engagements, sanctions, data, reports, and other necessary information. Media, including social media, is used extensively communicate these outputs with the public.

Ethics

OSIPTEL has an Institutional Code of Ethics, within the framework of the General Law on the Civil Service Code of Ethics (Law No. 27815) maintained by SERVIR. The Code contains five general dispositions and does not lay out supervisory and enforcement mechanisms. However, staff in violation of the code are subject to sanctions. Violations are reported to a designated person, who is currently the advisor to the President of the Board of Directors. This person accepts this responsibility on top of regular work duties. All violations are handled by an ethics committee, while severe violations are escalated to the Human Resources Manager. In severe cases such as corruption, the violation is escalated to the SERVIR tribunal, who will provide the appropriate sanction. Violations are not reported anonymously and, to date, there have been no violations ever reported.

An ethics working group, which includes a representative from each department, ensures that OSIPTEL staffs are aware of the code and promote ethical behaviour within the workplace. This is promoted through emails or during induction programs and institutional events. The ethics code is published on OSIPTEL's website for transparency, as well as posted in several areas around the OSIPTEL buildings.

Transparency

OSIPTEL operated an 'open-door' policy with regulated entities, allowing them to come to the regulator to discuss issues. Recent changes, however, restricted this access during the regulatory development phase, whereby regulated entities must wait until the public consultation to provide their inputs into draft laws.

According to OSIPTEL's rules on transparency, meetings with the operators' representatives must be documented on the OSIPTEL Transparency Portal and the Peruvian Government Transparency Portal, which displays the name of the entity and representatives visiting, a headline about the topic discussed, and the names of OSIPTEL staff met. A detailed description of what was discussed is not included.

Conflicts of interest

Conflict of interest guidelines, issued in 2018, sets the specific procedure and format to declare possible conflicts of interest.[20] These require all staff to declare any possible conflicts, including with family members or friends. This declaration needs to be updated yearly, or when major changes occur. This process is enforced by the GAL.

Post-employment restrictions are governed by Law 27588, which establishes prohibitions and behaviours that are incompatible for all staff qualified as civil servants. These rules apply to all people that provide civil services under any contractual arrangement. According to the Law, any board members, senior officials, advisors and members of administrative tribunals, as well as officers or public servants that have had access to privileged information or whose opinion has been determinant in decision making, are subject to a one-year post-employment restriction. This includes providing services under contractual arrangement, accepting remuneration, being part of the Board of Directors, directly or indirectly acquiring shares of a company associated with the sector, signing contracts with companies, or participating in employment with companies.

Likewise, OSIPTEL's General Regulation stipulates that board members, senior officials and servants despite their contractual arrangement are forbidden to defend or counsel any entity against OSIPTEL and to work for any institution within the jurisdiction of OSIPTEL for a year after ending their professional relationship with OSIPTEL.

Staff members subject to post-employment restrictions, which have ended their professional relationship with OSIPTEL, must sign a legal document committing not to violate the terms and conditions of the policy. OSIPTEL has stated that these provisions do cause some difficulty recruiting new personnel.

To avoid conflict of interest, any person who owns more than one per cent of shares of a company related to the competency of the regulator cannot be appointed as a member of the board or hired as a director, legal representative, agent, employee or consultant of a regulatory agency.

Conflict of Interest guidelines require Board members to declare any possible conflicts, including with family members or friends. This declaration needs to be updated yearly, or when major changes occur. This process is enforced by the Legal Advisory Department (*Gerencia Asesoría Legal*, GAL).

Output and outcome

Data collection

OSIPTEL collects a large amount of data from the regulated entities, which it uses to monitor market performance, detect market failures and develop regulations. This includes sector performance data, as well as financial data for the five biggest operators. Data is turned into indicators, which are presented to the Board. Non-confidential information is posted in its raw form on the OSIPTEL website.

Most data requests are part of the Periodic Information Requirements Rule (*Norma de Requerimientos de Información Periódica*, NRIP), which is sent through the Periodic Information System (*Sistema de gestión de las estadísticas periódicas,* SIGEP), which is a predictable and digital data collection tool that includes 185 forms. Companies may be requested to provide exceptional information in response to specific rules or in response to letters sent by the regulator, which are often based on information requests from other entities of the Peruvian executive branch or that are necessary by the OSIPTEL in a non-periodic way.

Regulated entities are often requested to provide detailed amount of data on the market. Conversely, the regulator sometimes finds that information that is submitted is incomplete, is not submitted on time, or is inconsistent (in the latter case, for example for the use of codes that do not match, atypical evolution of series, etc.). For most relevant indicators, a procedure has been implemented in order to detect inconsistent or incomplete information (evaluating the evolution of the time series, verifying blank cells, etc.). The process is currently done manually with database tools.

Smaller or newer entrants to the sector may identify issues in obtaining all data on a regular basis. However, larger firms may also submit inconsistent or incomplete data. Telefónica and Claro (*América Móvil*) are required to send additional periodic information on *inter alia* lines, subscriptions and data once a year to supplement the SIGEP data. This is due to the large impact of these firms in the sector.

OSIPTEL ensures that its data requests are reasonable and in line with actual data requirements to minimise burden on industry. This is done through regular reviews of data requests via the SIGEP that is administrated by the Regulatory Policy and Competition department (GPRC), or via other specific rules that are approved by each department. Each department is responsible for drafting indicators and collecting information for the PEI and POI reporting and monitoring. If data required is not collected through the NRIP, then each department requests the information via their own rule or by letter. In August 2018, OSIPTEL began a process to revise the SIGEP data requirements to reduce the number of formats in an effort to reduce burden on operators.

Box 2.4 describes the data collection channels of OSIPTEL. The regulator also has the ability to request specific information from companies if it is not already collected through any of the existing data collection efforts, as indicated in article 100 of the General Regulations of OSIPTEL.

Box 2.4. OSIPTEL data collection systems

Internally, the GRPC manages three main data collection systems that gather data on sector performance.

1. Periodic Information System (SIGEP)

The Periodic Information Requirements Rule (*Norma de Requerimientos de Información Periódica*, NRIP) includes a total of 185 forms that require information of lines, traffic, infrastructure, financial, and claim indicators. The NRIP was created on in 2004 and was digitised in 2015 through the Periodic Information System (*Sistema de gestión de las estadísticas periódicas*, SIGEP). The SIGEP is a predictable and digital data collection tool, used by the regulated entities for reporting that information; this System is also, a database of statistical information on the performance of the telecommunications sector.

The quality of data submitted via the SIGEP is ensured *inter alia* by blocking submissions if data cells are left blank.

Due to changing market dynamics, OSIPTEL recognises that the NRIP must improve its data collection forms and/or review collected information that is no longer utilised or relevant, to ensure that all data collected is used periodically by the regulator. Since this change requires a special regulation, it can be lengthy to modify NRIP requirements. In the interim, special information requirements are sent to regulated entities (such as market and infrastructure of the carrier service), which will be included in a new project of the NRIP. OSIPTEL is also working on a project to optimise the use of all data collected through the SIGEP system. The GPRC is designing indicators (graphs/tables) that are used frequently in different documents and will be made automatically through the system, therefore saving time.

2. Price Information System (SIRT)

The Price Information System (*Sistema de consultas de tarifas*, SIRT) requires operators to register the price of every commercial offer, which is then made publicly available on the OSIPTEL website. Promotions must be registered 24 hours before they are released to clients while price increases must be registered 15 days before it is applied to users.

This information is used to populate *Comparitel*, a website that allows consumers to compare offers of different operators, as well as find details about price increases and track the evolution of commercial offers. *Comparitel* can only compare current listed prices and not special offers.

3. Annual Consumer Demand Survey (ERESTEL)

The Annual Consumer Demand Survey (*Encuesta residencial de servicios de telecomunicaciones*, ERESTEL) asks a sample of 10 000 households about their use of services, preferences, attitudes towards switching, among others. All information about the survey, including surveying material is published on this OSIPTEL website, along with an analytical presentation of the year's results. 2016 results can be found here.

4. Other data collected

Other sources of information include internal reports on specific subjects, tariff benchmarks conducted biannually for some markets or services, statistics prepared by other regulators or international public bodies (i.e. Regulatel, CITEL, OECD, UIT), and information from other areas in OSIPTEL (claims, information from users drawn from the social networks) and / or stakeholders, which are mostly enterprises.

Operators are required to present quarterly information on the villages that have received coverage on or before the 15 of January, April, July and October. Regulated entities are also required to provide performance information related to call accessibility and retention of mobile voice service.

Radio network operators are required to produce information regarding their network measurements (counters). These counters are the base of Key Performance Indicators (KPI), which are used for measuring network performance.

Source: information provided by OSIPTEL, 2018; Resolution No. 121-2003-CD/OSIPTEL; Resolution 050-2012-CD/OSIPTEL; Resolution 096-2015-CD/OSIPTEL, Regulation on Tariffs (art. 11); Resolution No. 135-2013-CD/OSIPTEL; Resolution No. 123-2014-CD/OSIPTEL; Resolution No. 110-2015-CD/OSIPTEL.

Performance monitoring

OSIPTEL 2018-2022 PEI is structured along seven high-level strategic institutional objectives (OEIs), separated into four core (market outcome) and three support (process and output) objectives. Core objectives are related to the mission of the institution, whereas support objectives are related to the internal management and processes of OSIPTEL. The OEIs are measured via 21 mostly outcome-level indicators.

The PEI is translated into institutional strategic actions, according to each OEI. The four core OEIs are implemented via 16 priority actions, measured via 36 indicators; the three support OEIs via 14 priority actions and 32 indicators. Appropriately, the indicators at this level focus on input, process and output (see Table 2.19). The full table of institutional strategic actions in available in Annex 2.A (in Spanish). Targets for these indicators are not fixed in the PEI. MEF also requires OSIPTEL to share data to inform a set of indicators for monitoring budget execution and performance. These MEF indicators are not included in the strategic framework for the regulator.

The indicators used to monitor the implementation of the plan are aligned with the OEIs and include sophisticated indices constructed by the Regulatory Policy and Competition department (GPRC). Moreover, these indices are combined for higher level indicators such as the Competitive Intensity Index (*índice de intensidad competitiva*), which has been calculated since the first quarter of 2012.

The index is composed of indicators of the main unregulated services: pay TV market, fixed Internet market and mobile telephony market (see Figure 2.6). It is used to evaluate whether or not competition has increased with respect to the same quarter of the previous year. The construction of the sub-index for each market is composed of four weighted ratios: i) market concentration, ii) quality of service, iii) services prices and iv) lines in service.

Figure 2.6. Competitive intensity index

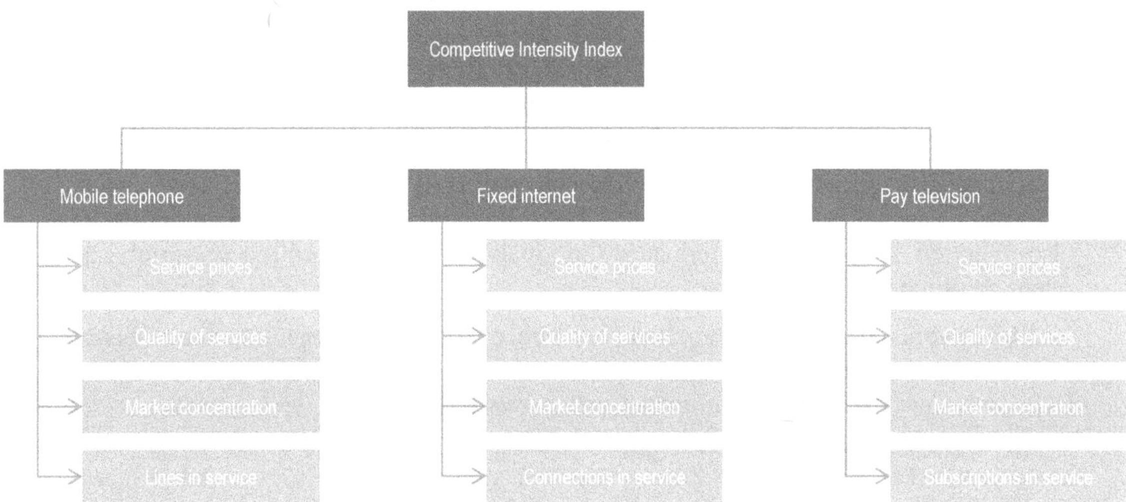

Source: Information provided by OSIPTEL, 2018.

The index has specific limitations. For example, only the indicators for voice services are considered in the mobile telephone market and not the indicators related to the mobile internet service. This is due to issues related to acquiring accurate information on mobile internet service, mainly regarding data traffic and income from the service. As a result, OSIPTEL is working with technical staff in the operators to improve the accuracy of this information and include it in the index. The operators have been progressively reporting improvements in their internal data systems and providing corrected data. In addition, OSIPTEL is focused on addressing monitoring challenges related to information on quality of services and is considering proxies to help measure the quality of services provided, such as speed as a proxy for internet service quality.

OSIPTEL will be implementing a second index that will measure quality in consumer service in all types of telecommunications services. In addition, a set of questionnaires are being prepared to gauge user satisfaction on services provided by the operator, in terms of its efficiency and effectiveness. The questionnaires will be administered through telephone, online and in person. They expect to have first results at the end of 2018.

OSIPTEL uses information collected to better diagnose problems in the market, assess its performance, and identify necessary modifications to current regulations or other measures to address any issues. Ad hoc market surveys help identify the impacts of some regulations. Other important statistics of the telecom market are also considered in market analyses, such as lines, market share, traffic, access, income of operators and industry as a whole, etc.

The 2018-2022 PEI includes a new project to integrate all databases and to make them accessible to all officials, with the exception of confidential data. This project brings together three internal committees (competition, quality and users), and expects to have results at the end of 2018.

Table 2.19. OSIPTEL strategic objectives and indicators, 2018-2022

Type	Strategic objective	Indicator	
Core	Promote competition between telecommunications operators	• Mobile telephony competition index • Mobile telephony price index • Mobile internet competition index • Mobile internet price index • Fixed internet competition index • Fixed internet price index • Pay TV competition index • Pay TV price index	*Outcome*
	Guarantee compliance with quality standards in telecommunications services, as established or offered by the operators	• Mobile telephony quality of service index • Mobile internet quality of service index • Fixed internet quality of service index • Pay TV quality of service index	*Outcome*
	Promote appropriate attention to users by operators	• % of compliance with quality of service standards in customer service by operators • % of user satisfaction with quality of customer service by operator	*Outcome*
	Empower telecommunications service users	• % of users who know they basic rights • % of users with problems with service who found an adequate solution	*Outcome*
Support	Consolidate OSIPTEL's reputation as a transparent and highly specialised institution	• OSIPTEL reputation index	*Process*
	Consolidate the management model of OSIPTEL towards excellence	• % of internal client satisfaction with Line Departments • % of internal client satisfaction with Support and Advisory Bodies • OSIPTEL management excellency index	*Process*
	Implement processes for disaster risk management	• Number of implementation or update reports for disaster risk management	*Output*

Source: OSIPTEL Strategic Plan 2018-2022.

Reporting

Autonomous regulatory authorities in Peru are only legally mandated to report to the Ministry of Economy and Finance, as part of Peru's administration-wide performance based budgeting system. OSIPTEL submits information on indicators that have been defined by MEF via the online integrated administrative financial system (*Sistemas integrados de administación financiera,* SIAF) every year. OSIPTEL also sends a hard copy of this report to its stakeholders in the executive (Comptroller) and legislative branches of government (Permanent Budget Committee of the Congress). The indicators reported in the SIAF to MEF are listed in Table 2.20.

Table 2.20. SAIF Indicators sent to MEF

Specific result / product	Name of indicator
RE: Improvement of the Provision of Telecommunications Services	User satisfaction level – Fixed Telephony User User satisfaction level – Mobile Telephony User User satisfaction level – Internet User User satisfaction level – Cable User
Product 1: Localities supervised according to technical service standards	Quality level of radio coverage of the mobile service Quality Index of mobile telephony Rate of solving detected non-compliances regarding Internet speed Percentage of compliance of minimum guaranteed Internet speed.
Product 2: Operators have mechanisms to provide tariff schemes accessible to user	Real Savings Amount accumulated in the Fixed Telephone Service Competition Index for TV Cable Competition Index for Internet Competition Index for Mobile Telephony Annual savings amount of for urban rural differentiated charges
Product 3: Users protected in their rights	User satisfaction Index regarding OSIPTEL orientation service Percentage of users knowing their rights.

Source: Information provided by OSIPTEL, 2018.

These indicators are not the similar to those defined by OSIPTEL for its strategic framework and priority actions, although there is some overlap. Combined with the strategic framework (21 indicators for the strategic objectives, 68 indicators for priority actions), OSIPTEL performance is reported on via 104 indicators.

PCM and Congress also regularly request presentations of result indicators and targets, which are those designed within the framework of the Budget Program and incorporated in the POI for follow-up. The level of compliance with these goals is reported by semester, according to the programmatic functional structure approved for each fiscal year.

The OCI also produces an audit of the POI to be submitted to the Supreme Audit Institution. Each department at OSIPTEL is responsible for constructing their relevant indicators and building an index from the data, without requesting additional information and indicators are approved by MEF. The PPR is reviewed each year, which also requires an evaluation of the indicators being used. Reports to MEF and the OCI are processed online.

Once a year, as required by law, OSIPTEL prepares an annual report on its main activities and results. The reports are comprehensive, insightful, easy-to-read and well-produced, and are made available online.[21] There is no particular requirement to share these reports with Congress or any other stakeholder, nor does OSIPTEL organise any physical presentation event of the report. However, OSIPTEL may be invited to congressional meetings to address specific matters, concerning tariff provisions, budget, or other relevant issues. These requests are normally made by the Defense of Consumers and Regulatory Bodies Commission (CODECO) and attended by the President of the Board or General Manager, who present the requested information or respond to questions raised.

A large amount of raw data is also made available in OSIPTEL's website, for example:

- Data on the performance of the markets that it oversees;[22]
- Data from its yearly consumer survey.[23]

Based on this data, OSIPTEL prepares and communicates analysis via varied and extensive outputs that may be one-off or part of a series. These include:

- Two- to three-page statistical reports on the evolution of the telecommunications sector, principally on the mobile telephony market and coverage on its website every one to three months. These reports provide snapshots into the performance of different areas under OSIPTEL's responsibility[24] and include the following:
    - Quarterly statistics: general and specific information on mobile, fixed, internet, or paid TV services, penetration, traffic, market share, income, and financial statements for largest service providers, etc.
    - Characteristics of the plans offered by telecommunication firms
    - Main changes in the telecommunications market
- Newsletters on a quarterly basis that include a preface from the Chairman of the board and present major evolutions in the telecommunications market as well as customer preferences.[25]
- Working papers on thematic topics that inform the development of indicators, for example on bundled fixed services and mobile telephony in 2017), (such as statistical reports published every 2-3 months).
- Internally, OSIPTEL prepares quarterly reports on the implementation of the POI that are presented to the Board of directors. These reports are not made public.

Notes

[1] Articles 85 and 86 of the Single Consolidated Text (TUO) of Law No. 27444, General Administrative Procedure Act, approved by Supreme Decree No. 006-2017-JUS.

[2] Governed by Law No. 29571 or the Consumer Protection and Defense Code, passed in 2010.

[3] Approved by Supreme Decree No. 008-2001-PCM.

[4] Article 1 of Supreme Decree No. 098-2016-PCM.

[5] See: Ley de Equilibrio Financiero de Presupuesto del Sector Publico Para el Año 2018, https://www.mef.gob.pe/es/por-instrumento/ley/16769-ley-n-30694/file.

[6] In 2007, the Government of Peru, through MEF, implemented a budget for results system, initially called "Strategic Programming and measurement of results"; the strategic programmes prioritised were those that provided care for children, such as: i) Maternal and Neonatal Health, ii) Nutritional Articulation, iii) Achievements of Learning at the end of the third cycle, iv) Population Access to Identity, and v) Access to Basic Social Services and Market Opportunities. Government Entities that would attend the selected programs were: i) Ministry of Education, ii) Ministry of Health, iii) Ministry of Women and Social Development and IV) Ministry of Transports and Communications. OSIPTEL is integrated into the Budget for Results in 2015 with its programme named No. 0124 Improvement of the Provision of Telecommunications Services.

[7] The SIAF allows OSIPTEL to manage, improve and supervise the revenue and expenditure operations of all State Entities, as well as allowing the integration of the budgetary, accounting and treasury processes of each entity. This system is of mandatory use for Public Sector Entities according to the Framework Law of the Financial Administration of the Public Sector.

[8] The SAI is designed for internal use by OSIPTEL in order to have an updated system that supports the processes and information needs, and to simplify processes for information analysis to facilitate management. The SAI is interfaced with the SIAF for the exchange of information.

[9] Law No. 28212, in accordance with Supreme Decree No. 046-2006-PCM, approved new remuneration caps for the public sector. Emergency Decree 038-2006, which modified Law 28121, reduced the remuneration for the President and Managers of regulatory bodies.

[10] Supreme Decree No. 172-2013-EF.

[11] Law No. 27332, art. 10.

[12] The Guidelines were approved under Resolution 069-2018-CD/OSIPTEL.

[13] Lineamientos para Desarrollar y Consolidar la Competencia y la Expansion de los servicios de Telecomunicaciones en el Peru – DS 003-2007-MTC.

[14] Memorando 047-GAL/2018 contains a schedule of activities for this evaluation.

[15] Laws No. 27332 *Regulatory Agencies Framework Law* and No. 27336 *Functions and Faculties of Supervisory Agency for Private Investment in Telecommunications Law.*

[16] The first law was the "Directive that defines the framework to establish the procedures associated with the complaints of users of public telecommunications services", approved by Resolution of OSIPTEL's Board of Directors No. 007-94-CD/OSIPTEL. After that, there were two more Resolutions approved by the OSIPTEL's Board of Directors that regulated the complaint procedure: No. 032-97-CD/OSIPTEL and 015-99-CD/OSIPTEL. Then, the OSIPTEL's Presidency approved the Resolution No. 036-97-PD/OSIPTEL as well.

[17] Regulation for the Attention of Complaints of Users of Public Telecommunications Services" (hereinafter, referred as the Regulation of Complaints), approved by the Resolution of OSIPTEL's Board of Directors No. 047-2015-CD/OSIPTEL. The Regulation of Complaints has been modified by the Resolution of OSIPTEL's Board of Directors No. 127-2016-CD/OSIPTEL, in 2016; by the Resolution of OSIPTEL's Board of Directors No. 048-2017-CD/OSIPTEL, in 2017; and by the Resolution of OSIPTEL's Board of Directors No. 051-2018-CD/OSIPTEL, in 2018.

[18] Article 7 of the General Regulations of OSIPTEL.

[19] Under Article 33 of Law No. 27336 or the Law of Development of Functions and Powers.

[20] https://www.osiptel.gob.pe/articulo/res101-2018-cd-osiptel.

[21] Annual reports can be found at www.osiptel.gob.pe/documentos/memorias-anuales.

[22] https://www.osiptel.gob.pe/documentos/indicadores-estadisticos.

[23] https://www.osiptel.gob.pe/documentos/encuesta-residencial-erestel.

[24] For full list, see: www.osiptel.gob.pe/documentos/reporte-estadistico.

[25] www.osiptel.gob.pe/documentos/boletin-osiptelcom.

References

El Comercio (2015), *VisaNet, Liderman y Cofide ganan el Great Place to Work | Economía | Perú | El Comercio Perú*, https://elcomercio.pe/economia/peru/visanet-liderman-cofide-ganan-great-place-to-work-205562?foto=2 (accessed on 22 June 2018). [4]

OECD (2016), *OECD Public Governance Reviews: Peru: Integrated Governance for Inclusive Growth*, OECD Public Governance Reviews, OECD Publishing, Paris, http://dx.doi.org/10.1787/9789264265172-en. [3]

OECD (2016), *Regulatory Policy in Peru: Assembling the Framework for Regulatory Quality*, OECD Reviews of Regulatory Reform, OECD Publishing, Paris, http://dx.doi.org/10.1787/9789264260054-en. [2]

OSIPTEL (2018), *Plan Estratégico Institucional 2018-22*, OSIPTEL, https://www.osiptel.gob.pe/repositorioaps/data/1/1/1/PAR/res025-2018-pd/Res025-2018-PD_PEI2018-2022.pdf (accessed on 22 June 2018). [1]

OSIPTEL (2014), *The Telecommunications Boom*, OSIPTEL, https://www.osiptel.gob.pe/Archivos/Publicaciones/boom_telecomunicaciones/boom_telecomunicaciones_osiptel.html#6. [5]

Annex 2.A. OSIPTEL Institutional Strategic Plan (PEI), 2018-2022

COD	Acción estratégica	Indicador
OEI.01 Promover la competencia entre empresas operadoras de servicios de telecomunicaciones		
AEI.01.01	Vigilancia y análisis del mercado de telecomunicaciones implementado para el beneficio de los usuarios el beneficio de los usuarios.	% herramientas de fortalecimiento del sistema de vigilancia de promoción de la competencia implementadas y/o mejoradas % de herramientas de vigilancia de promoción de competencia con efectividad en su uso % de problemas de competencia analizados de manera oportuna
AEI.01.02	Políticas y estrategias formuladas e implementadas para promover la competencia entre empresas operadoras	% de problemas de competencia analizados que cuentan con políticas y/o estrategias definidas. % de normas emitidas y/o actualizadas bajo estándares RIA
AEI.01.03	Marco normativo actualizado bajo estándares RIA para beneficio del Mercado de telecomunicaciones	% de normas cuya eficacia se evaluó bajo estándares RIA % de normas evaluadas que califican como eficaces
AEI.01.04	Supervisión del Mercado de telecomunicaciones de manera oportuna	% de supervisiones de competencia ejecutados en plazo % de controversias resueltas en un plazo menor al establecido
AEI.01.05	Solución de controversias de libre y leal competencia eficiente y oportuna para las empresas operadoras	% de puntos de las resoluciones de los Cuerpos Colegiados confirmadas en segunda instancia % de Informes de Investigación Preliminar efectivos.
OEI.02 Garantizar el cumplimiento de los estándares de calidad de los servicios de telecomunicaciones establecidos en relación a lo ofrecido por las empresas operadoras.		
AEI.02.01	Vigilancia y análisis de la calidad de la prestación de los servicios de telecomunicaciones implementado para beneficio de los usuarios.	% herramientas de fortalecimiento del sistema de vigilancia de calidad de prestación implementadas y/o mejoradas % de herramientas de vigilancia de la calidad de prestación de los servicios con efectividad en su uso % de problemas de calidad de prestación de servicios de telecomunicaciones analizados oportunamente
AEI.02.02	Estándares de calidad adecuada ofrecidos a los usuarios de servicios de telecomunicaciones.	% de problemas de calidad de los servicios de telecomunicaciones que cuentan con estándares definidos y/o revisados
AEI.02.03	Monitoreo, compromisos de mejora, supervisión y fiscalización eficaz de la calidad de la prestación de los servicios de telecomunicaciones.	% de monitoreos que generaron soluciones % de supervisiones que generaron correcciones durante la supervisión % de compromisos de mejora de las empresas operadoras ejecutadas % de medidas dictadas en el proceso de fiscalización cumplidas
OEI.03 Promover la atención adecuada de los usuarios por parte de las empresas operadoras de servicios de telecomunicaciones.		
AEI.03.01	Vigilancia y análisis de los problemas que tienen los usuarios de los servicios de telecomunicación implementada.	% herramientas de fortalecimiento del sistema de vigilancia de problemas de usuarios implementadas y/o mejoradas

COD	Acción estratégica	Indicador
		% de herramientas de vigilancia de calidad de atención a los usuarios con efectividad en su uso
		% de problemas de calidad de atención a los usuarios, analizados oportunamente
AEI.03.02	Políticas y estrategias formuladas e implementadas para proteger al usuario de servicios de telecomunicaciones.	% de problemas de calidad de atención a usuarios que cuentan políticas y/o estrategias definidas.
AEI.03.03	Supervisión de la calidad de atención a usuarios de los servicios de telecomunicaciones, brindados de manera oportuna.	% de supervisiones de calidad de atención a usuarios, ejecutados en plazo
OEI.04 Empoderar a los usuarios de servicios de telecomunicaciones.		
AEI.04.01	Información para la toma de decisiones, actualizada en beneficio de los usuarios de los servicios de telecomunicaciones.	% de herramientas informáticas puestas a disposición de los usuarios de los servicios de telecomunicaciones implementados y/o mejorados.
		% de usuarios que compararon entre planes y/o empresas operadoras antes de contratar
		Nº de canales de información puesta a disposición de los usuarios.
AEI.04.02	Intervención en el proceso de solución de reclamos de usuarios, eficaz para beneficio de los usuarios de los servicios de telecomunicaciones.	% de soluciones anticipadas de reclamos favorables al usuario
		% de reclamos fundados en primera instancia
		% de soluciones anticipadas de recursos de apelación
AEI.04.03	Solución de quejas y apelaciones efectivo para el beneficio de los usuarios.	% de denuncias en las que se acreditó el cumplimiento de la empresa operadora
		% de resoluciones del TRASU cumplidas
		% de recursos de apelación resueltos en segunda instancia dos días antes del plazo establecido
AEI.04.04	Orientación efectiva a los usuarios de los servicios de telecomunicaciones.	% de usuarios satisfechos con el servicio de orientación brindado por el OSIPTEL
AEI.04.05	Educación especializada en derechos y deberes para los usuarios de los servicios públicos de telecomunicaciones.	% de usuarios satisfechos con los servicios de educación brindados por el OSIPTEL.
		% de usuarios evaluados satisfactoriamente con los servicios de educación brindados por el OSIPTEL.
OEI.05 Consolidar la reputación en alta especialización y transparencia.		
AEI.05.01	Estrategias de comunicación diferenciadas por cada stakeholder.	% de estrategias de comunicación diseñadas para cada stakeholder
		% de cumplimiento de las actividades de las estrategias de comunicación diferenciadas por stakeholder
AEI.05.02	Procesos y sentencias judiciales con resultados favorables para el OSIPTEL.	% de procesos concluidos en el año
		% de procesos judiciales concluidos a favor del OSIPTEL en el año
		% de sentencias obtenidas a favor del OSIPTEL en el año
AEI.05.03	Intercambio eficaz de buenas prácticas de gestión con actores internacionales.	% de buenas prácticas identificadas como replicables en la Institución
		% de espacios (*) en los que el OSIPTEL presenta su experiencia de gestión. * Por "espacios" se entiende a talleres, exposiciones, presentaciones y pasantías
OEI.06 Consolidar el modelo de excelencia en la gestión institucional.		
AEI.06.01	Planeamiento estratégico eficiente del OSIPTEL.	% de ejecución de las metas del PEI programadas.
		% de metas programadas modificadas
AEI.06.02	Presupuesto gestionado por resultados, implementado y programado por prioridades en el OSIPTEL.	% de certificaciones presupuestales aprobadas
		Índice de eficiencia de ejecución de recursos financieros

COD	Acción estratégica	Indicador
AEI.06.03	Gestión por Procesos implementado en el OSIPTEL.	% de procesos clave rediseñados y alineados al PEI
		% de procesos clave rediseñados e incorporados al ISO
AEI.06.04	TICs integrados que soportan el negocio institucional.	% de soluciones tecnológicas implementadas a disposición de los usuarios internos
		% de sistemas integrados
		% de procesos que se encuentran sistematizados
		% de requerimientos de las áreas usuarias atendidas en plazo
AEI.06.05	Gestión de la innovación y modelos de mejora continua eficaces para beneficio del OSIPTEL.	% del personal que participa en la gestión de la innovación del Osiptel.
		% de iniciativas desarrolladas que son implementadas por las Unidades Orgánicas en su gestión.
AEI.06.06	Gestión de riesgos controlados para el OSIPTEL.	% de riesgos altos y extremos institucionales sobre los cuales se han tomado acciones
AEI.06.07	Gestión del conocimiento implementado en el OSIPTEL.	% del sistema de gestión del conocimiento implementado
		% del personal identificado como generador de conocimiento que incorpora activos de conocimiento al sistema
		% de activos de conocimiento actualizados y valorados
		% del personal que accede al sistema de gestión del conocimiento
AEI.06.08	Fortalecimiento de capacidades de los recursos humanos del OSIPTEL.	Índice de clima laboral
		% de colaboradores que incrementaron su promedio en la evaluación de desempeño
AEI.06.09	Gestión financiera sostenible del OSIPTEL.	% de aportes recaudados dentro del plazo de vencimiento
		% de empresas operadoras que han presentado su declaración jurada anual de ingresos percibidos y facturados
		% de requerimientos contratados a tiempo y de forma completa dentro del tiempo estándar establecido
OEI.07 Implementar la gestión de riesgo de desastres.		
AEI.07.01	Sistema de preparación ante emergencia por desastres de manera oportuna para el OSIPTEL.	Nº de informes de preparación del personal para casos de emergencia por desastres.
AEI.07.02	Plan de acción para la gestión de riesgos de desastres de manera oportuna para el OSIPTEL.	Nº de planes de acción formuladas y/o actualizadas para la gestión de riesgo de desastres.

Source: Information provided by OSIPTEL, 2018.

Annex 2.B. Application of RIA on cap tariffs and interconnection charges

Rules with RIA	Resolution (Draft / Final)	Publication date	Method Used	Link Web (Reports)
Modification of the General Regulation of Rates	Draft: Resolution No. 074-2016-CD/OSIPTEL	13.06.2016	Multi-criteria analysis	http://www.osiptel.gob.pe/repositorioaps/data/1/1/1/PAR/074-2016-cd-osiptel/Informe229-GPRC-2016_Resolucion074-2016-CD-OSIPTEL.pdf
Network Neutrality Regulation	Final: Resolution No. 165-2016-CD/OSIPTEL	21.12.2016	Qualitative analysis of costs and benefits	http://www.osiptel.gob.pe/repositorioaps/data/1/1/1/PAR/res165-2016-cd/Res165-2016-CD_Inf400-GPRC-2016.pdf
Review of the Cap Interconnection Charge for Access to the Payment Platform	Final: Resolution No. 024-2017-CD/OSIPTEL	25.02.2017	Qualitative analysis of costs and benefits	http://www.osiptel.gob.pe/repositorioaps/data/1/1/1/PAR/res024-2017-cd/Res024-2017-CD_Inf028-GPRC-2017.pdf
Review of the Cap Interconnection Charge for Billing and Collection	Final: Resolution No. 030-2017-CD/OSIPTEL	13.03.2017	Qualitative analysis of costs and benefits	http://www.osiptel.gob.pe/repositorioaps/data/1/1/1/PAR/res030-2017-cd/Res030-2017-CD_Inf038-GPRC-2017.pdf
Complementary Rules applicable to Rural Mobile Infrastructure Operators	Final: Resolution No. 059-2017-CD/OSIPTEL	28.04.2017	Multi-criteria analysis	http://www.osiptel.gob.pe/repositorioaps/data/1/1/1/PAR/res059-2017-cd/Res059-2017-CD_Inf074-GPRC-2017.pdf
Complementary Rules for the implementation of the RENTESEG	Final: Resolution No. 081-2017-CD/OSIPTEL	13.07.2017	Multi-criteria analysis	http://www.osiptel.gob.pe/repositorioaps/data/1/1/1/PAR/res081-2017-cd/Res081-2017-CD_Inf138-GPRC-2017.pdf
Determination of the Important Supplier: Markets No. 22, 23 and 24 (Wholesale Service of Lease of Local Circuits, NLD and ILD)	Draft: Resolution No. 124-2017-CD/OSIPTEL	27.10.2017	Qualitative analysis of costs and benefits	http://www.osiptel.gob.pe/repositorioaps/data/1/1/1/PAR/res124-2017-cd/Res124-2017-CD_Inf184-GPRC-2017.pdf
Rate System of Pay TV Service	Draft: Resolution No. 159-2017-CD/OSIPTEL	23.12.2017	Qualitative analysis of costs and benefits	http://www.osiptel.gob.pe/repositorioaps/data/1/1/1/PAR/res159-2017-cd/Res159-2017-CD_Inf223-GPRC-2017.pdf

Rules with RIA	Resolution (Draft / Final)	Publication date	Method Used	Link Web (Reports)
Modification of the Number Portability Regulation	Draft: Resolution No. 158-2017-CD/OSIPTEL	23.12.2017	Multi-criteria analysis	http://www.osiptel.gob.pe/repositorioaps/data/1/1/1/PAR/res158-2017-cd/Res158-2017-CD_Inf192-GPRC-2017.pdf
Review of the Cap Interconnection Charge for Termination Calls in Mobile Networks	Final: Resolution No. 021-2018-CD/OSIPTEL	28.01.2018	Qualitative analysis of costs and benefits	http://www.osiptel.gob.pe/repositorioaps/data/1/1/1/PAR/res021-2018-cd/05-Res021-2017-CD_Inf016-GPRC-2018.pdf
Determination of the Important Supplier: Markets No. 30 (access to the Mobile Network) y No. 33 (access to the Service from Mobiles)	Draft: Resolution No. 024-2018-CD/OSIPTEL	01.02.2018	Qualitative analysis of costs and benefits	http://www.osiptel.gob.pe/repositorioaps/data/1/1/1/PAR/res024-2018-cd/res024-2018-cd_inf229-gprc-2018.pdf
Modification of the methodology and rules for the Determination of Differentiated Interconnection Charges	Final: Resolution No. 038-2018-CD/OSIPTEL	16.02.2018	Multi-criteria analysis	http://www.osiptel.gob.pe/repositorioaps/data/1/1/1/PAR/res038-2018-cd/Res038-2018-CD_Inf008-GPRC-2018.pdf

Note: Rules approved by the Board of Directors.
Source: Information provided by OSIPTEL, 2018.

Annex A. Methodology

Measuring regulatory performance is challenging, starting with defining what to measure, dealing with confounding factors, attributing outcomes to interventions and coping with the lack of data and information. This chapter describes the methodology developed by the OECD to help regulators address these challenges through a Performance Assessment Framework for Economic Regulators (PAFER), which informs this review. The chapter first presents some of the work conducted by the OECD on measuring regulatory performance. It then describes the key features of the PAFER and presents a typology of performance indicators to measure input, process, output and outcome. It finally provides an overview of the approach and practical steps undertaken for developing this review.

Analytical framework

The analytical framework that informs this review draws on the work conducted by the OECD on measuring regulatory performance and the governance of economic regulators. OECD countries and regulators have recognised the need for measuring regulatory performance. Information on regulatory performance is necessary to better target scarce resources and to improve the overall performance of regulatory policies and regulators. However, measuring regulatory performance can prove challenging. Some of these challenges include:

- *What to measure*: evaluation systems require an assessment of how inputs have influenced outputs and outcomes. In the case of regulatory policy, the inputs can focus on: i) overall programmes intended to promote a systemic improvement of regulatory quality; ii) the application of specific practices intended to improve regulation, or, iii) changes in the design of specific regulations.
- *Confounding factors*: there is a myriad of contingent issues that have an impact on the outcomes in society which regulation is intended to affect. These issues can be as simple as a change in the weather, or as complicated as the last financial crisis. Accordingly, it is difficult to establish a direct causal relationship between the adoption of better regulation practices and specific improvements to the welfare outcomes that are sought in the economy.
- *Lack of data and information*: countries tend to lack data and methodologies to identify whether regulatory practices are being undertaken correctly and what impact these practices may be having on the real economy.

The OECD (2014[1]) *Framework for Regulatory Policy Evaluation* starts addressing these challenges through an input-process-output-outcome logic, which breaks down the regulatory process into a sequence of discrete steps. The input-process-output-outcome logic is flexible and can be applied both to evaluate practices to improve regulatory policy in general, and also to evaluate regulatory policy in specific sectors, based on the identification of relevant strategic objectives. It can be tailored to economic regulators by taking into consideration the conditions that support the performance of economic regulators (Box A A.1).

The OECD Best Practice Principles for Regulatory Policy: The Governance of Regulators (OECD, 2014[2]) identifies some of the conditions that support the performance of economic regulators. They recognise the importance of assessing how a regulator is directed, controlled, resourced and held to account, in order to improve the overall effectiveness of regulators and promote growth and investment, including by supporting competition. Moreover, they acknowledge the positive impact of the regulator's own internal process on outcomes (i.e. how the regulator manages resources and what processes the regulator puts in place to regulate a given sector or market) (Figure A A.1).

Box A A.1. The input-process-output-outcome logic sequence

- Step I. Input: indicators include for example the budget and staff of the regulatory oversight body.
- Step II. Process: indicators assess whether formal requirements for good regulatory practices are in place. This includes requirements for objective setting, consultation, evidence-based analysis, administrative simplification, risk assessments and aligning regulatory changes internationally.
- Step III. Output: indicators provide information on whether the good regulatory practices have actually been implemented.
- Step IV. Impact of design on outcome (also referred to as intermediate outcome): indicators assess whether good regulatory practices contributed to an improvement in the quality of regulations. It therefore attempts to make a causal link between the design of regulatory policy and outcomes.
- Step V. Strategic outcomes: indicators assess whether the desired outcomes of regulatory policy have been achieved, both in terms of regulatory quality and in terms of regulatory outcomes.

Source: (OECD, 2014[1]).

Figure A A.1. The OECD Best Practice Principles on the Governance of Regulators

Source: Adapted from (OECD, 2014[2]).

The two frameworks are brought together into a Performance Assessment Framework for Economic Regulators that structures the drivers of performance along the input-process-output-outcome framework (Table A A.1).

Table A A.1. Criteria for assessing regulators' own performance framework

References	Strategic objectives	Input	Process	Output and outcome
Best Practice Principles for the Governance of Regulators	• Role clarity	• Funding	• Maintaining trust and preventing undue influence • Decision making and governing body structure • Accountability and transparency • Engagement	• Performance evaluation
Institutional, organisational and monitoring drivers?	• Objectives and targets • Functions and powers	• Budgeting and financial management • Human resources management	• Strategy, leadership and co-ordination • Institutional structure • Management systems and operating processes • Relations and interfaces with Government bodies, regulated entities and other key stakeholders • Regulatory management tools	• Performance standards and indicators • Performance processes and reports • Feedback or outside evidence on performance

Source: OECD Analysis.

Performance indicators

For regulators, performance indicators need to fit the purpose of performance assessment, which is a systematic, analytical evaluation of the regulator's activities, with the purpose of seeking reliability and usability of the regulator's activities. Performance assessment is neither an audit, which judges how employees and managers complete their mission, nor a control, which puts emphasis on compliance with standards (OECD, 2004[3]).

Accordingly, performance indicators need to assess the efficient and effective use of a regulator's inputs, the quality of regulatory processes, and identify outputs and some direct outcomes that can be attributed to the regulator's interventions. Wider outcomes should serve as a "watchtower", which provides the information the regulator can use to identify problem areas, orient decisions and identify priorities (Figure A A.1).

Figure A A.2. Input-process-output-outcome framework for performance indicators

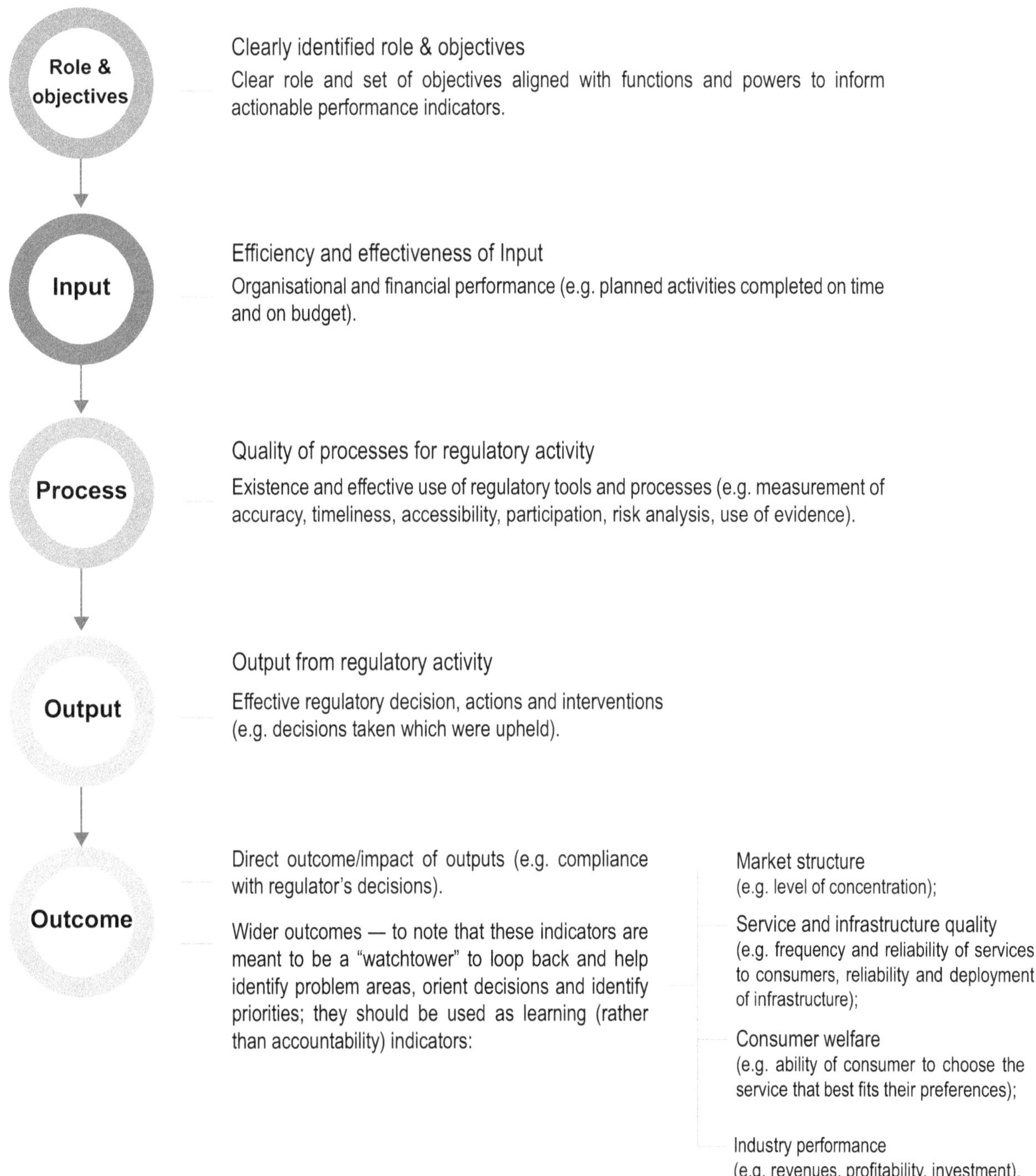

Notes: This framework was proposed in the initial methodology for the performance assessment framework for economic regulators (PAFER) discussed with the OECD Network of Economic Regulators (NER). It has been refined to reflect feedback from NER members and the experience of other regulators in assessing their own performance.
Source: (OECD, 2015[4]), Figure 3.3 (updated in 2017).

Approach

The analytical framework presented above informed the data collection and the analysis presented in the report. The present report looks at the internal and external governance arrangements of Peru's Supervisory Agency for Private Investment in Telecommunications (*Organismo Supervisor de Inversión Privada en Telecomunicaciones*, OSIPTEL) in the following areas:

- ***Strategic objectives***: to identify the existence of a set of clearly identified objectives, targets, or goals that are aligned with the regulator's functions and powers, which can inform the development of actionable performance indicators;
- ***Input***: to determine the extent to which the regulator's funding and staffing are aligned with the regulator's objectives, targets or goals, and the regulator's ability to manage financial and human resources autonomously and effectively;
- ***Process***: to assess the extent to which processes and the organisational management support the regulator's performance;
- ***Output and outcome***: to identify the existence of a systematic assessment of the performance of the regulated entities, the impact of the regulator's decisions and activities, and the extent to which these measurements are used appropriately.

Data informing the analysis presented in the report was collected via a desk review, a fact-finding mission and a peer mission to Peru:

- ***Questionnaire and desk review***: OSIPTEL completed a detailed questionnaire which informed a desk review by the OECD Secretariat. The Secretariat reviewed existing legislation and OSIPTEL documents to collect information on the *de jure* functioning of the regulator, and to inform the basis of the fact-finding mission. This questionnaire was tailored to OSIPTEL, based on the methodology already applied by the OECD to Colombia's Communications Regulation commission (OECD, 2015[4]), Latvia's Public Utilities Commission (OECD, 2016[5]), Mexico's three energy regulators (OECD, 2017[6]); (OECD, 2017[7]); (OECD, 2017[8]); (OECD, 2017[9]) and Ireland's Commission for Regulation of Utilities (OECD, 2018[10]). A series of one-on-one meetings took place on 13-15 February 2018 in Lima with the various teams responsible for completing the questionnaire, which coincided with the kick off of the review process.
- ***Fact-finding mission***: the mission was conducted by the OECD Secretariat on 14-17 May 2018 in Lima and was the key tool to collect and complete the *de jure* information obtained through the questionnaire with the *de facto* state of play. The work of the fact-finding mission tailored the PAFER methodology to OSIPTEL features. Information collected was completed and checked with OSIPTEL for accuracy, and issues for further discussion were also flagged.
- ***Peer mission***: the mission took place on 11-14 September 2018 in Lima and included peer reviewers in addition to OECD Secretariat. This mission took place concurrently with the peer mission for the PAFER review of Peru's Supervisory Agency for Investment in Energy and Mining (*Organismo Supervisor de la Inversión en Energía y Minería,* Osinergmin), which helped the peer mission team understand the systemic issues facing regulatory authorities in Peru. This mission met with key stakeholders in OSIPTEL as well as externally. At the end of the mission, the team discussed preliminary findings and recommendations

jointly with senior management from OSIPTEL and Osinergmin to test their feasibility and goodness of fit.

During the fact-finding and peer missions, the team met with OSIPTEL's leadership team as well as a number of staff from across the institution, other government institutions and external stakeholders, including:

- Agency for the Promotion of Investment (*Agencia de Promoción de la Inversión Privada,* ProInversión)
- Commission for Consumer Defence and Regulators of Public Utilities (*Comisión Defensa del Consumidor y Organismos Reguladores de los Servicios Públicos*, CODECO)
- National Institute for the Defense of Competition and Intellectual Property (*Instituto Nacional de Defensa de la Competencia y Protección de la Propiedad Intelectual*, Indecopi)
- Ministry of Economy and Finance (*Ministerio de Economía y Finanzas*, MEF)
- Ministry of Transport and Communications (*Ministerio de Tranporte y Comunicaciones*, MTC)
- National Centre for Strategic Planning (*Centro Nacional de Planeamiento estratégico*, CEPLAN)
- Presidency of the Council of Ministers (*Presidencia del Consejo de Ministros*, PCM)
- Peruvian Association of Consumers and Users (*Asociación Peruana de Consumidores y Usuarios*, ASPEC)
- Telecommunications Investment Fund (*Fondo de Inversión en Telecomunicaciones*, FITEL)
- America Movil Perú S.A. (*Claro*)
- Entel Perú S.A.
- Telefonica del Perú S.A.A
- Viettel Perú S.A.C.

References

OECD (2018), *Driving Performance at Ireland's Commission for Regulation of Utilities*, The Governance of Regulators, OECD Publishing, Paris, http://dx.doi.org/10.1787/9789264190061-en. [10]

OECD (2017), *Driving Performance at Mexico's Agency for Safety, Energy and Environment*, The Governance of Regulators, OECD Publishing, Paris, https://dx.doi.org/10.1787/9789264280458-en. [9]

OECD (2017), *Driving Performance at Mexico's Energy Regulatory Commission*, The Governance of Regulators, OECD Publishing, Paris, https://dx.doi.org/10.1787/9789264280830-en. [7]

OECD (2017), *Driving Performance at Mexico's National Hydrocarbons Commission*, The Governance of Regulators, OECD Publishing, Paris, https://dx.doi.org/10.1787/9789264280748-en. [8]

OECD (2017), *Driving Performance of Mexico's Energy Regulators*, The Governance of Regulators, OECD Publishing, Paris, https://dx.doi.org/10.1787/9789264267848-en. [6]

OECD (2016), *Driving Performance at Latvia's Public Utilities Commission*, The Governance of Regulators, OECD Publishing, Paris, https://dx.doi.org/10.1787/9789264257962-en. [5]

OECD (2015), *Driving Performance at Colombia's Communications Regulator*, OECD Publishing, Paris, https://dx.doi.org/10.1787/9789264232945-en. [4]

OECD (2014), *OECD Framework for Regulatory Policy Evaluation*, OECD Publishing, Paris, https://dx.doi.org/10.1787/9789264214453-en. [1]

OECD (2014), *The Governance of Regulators*, OECD Best Practice Principles for Regulatory Policy, OECD Publishing, Paris, https://dx.doi.org/10.1787/9789264209015-en. [2]

OECD (2004), *The choice of tools for enhancing policy impact: Evaluation and review*, OECD, Paris, http://www.oecd.org/officialdocuments/publicdisplaydocumentpdf/?cote=gov/pgc(2004)4&doclanguage=en (accessed on 16 November 2018). [3]

ORGANISATION FOR ECONOMIC CO-OPERATION AND DEVELOPMENT

The OECD is a unique forum where governments work together to address the economic, social and environmental challenges of globalisation. The OECD is also at the forefront of efforts to understand and to help governments respond to new developments and concerns, such as corporate governance, the information economy and the challenges of an ageing population. The Organisation provides a setting where governments can compare policy experiences, seek answers to common problems, identify good practice and work to co-ordinate domestic and international policies.

The OECD member countries are: Australia, Austria, Belgium, Canada, Chile, the Czech Republic, Denmark, Estonia, Finland, France, Germany, Greece, Hungary, Iceland, Ireland, Israel, Italy, Japan, Korea, Latvia, Lithuania, Luxembourg, Mexico, the Netherlands, New Zealand, Norway, Poland, Portugal, the Slovak Republic, Slovenia, Spain, Sweden, Switzerland, Turkey, the United Kingdom and the United States. The European Union takes part in the work of the OECD.

OECD Publishing disseminates widely the results of the Organisation's statistics gathering and research on economic, social and environmental issues, as well as the conventions, guidelines and standards agreed by its members.

OECD PUBLISHING, 2, rue André-Pascal, 75775 PARIS CEDEX 16
(42 2018 56 1 P) ISBN 978-92-64-31049-0 – 2019

www.ingramcontent.com/pod-product-compliance
Lightning Source LLC
LaVergne TN
LVHW081408110826
845149LV00010B/1668

9789264310490